INTRODUCING
ISSUES WITH
OPPOSING
VIEWPOINTS®

The Music Industry

Jill Hamilton, *Book Editor*

GREENHAVEN PRESS
A part of Gale, Cengage Learning

GALE
CENGAGE Learning™

Detroit • New York • San Francisco • New Haven, Conn • Waterville, Maine • London

Christine Nasso, *Publisher*
Elizabeth Des Chenes, *Managing Editor*

For more information, contact:
Greenhaven Press
27500 Drake Rd.
Farmington Hills, MI 48331-3535
Or you can visit our Internet site at gale.cengage.com

For product information and technology assistance, contact us at

Gale Customer Support, 1-800-877-4253
For permission to use material from this text or product, submit all requests online at www.cengage.com/permissions

Further permissions questions can be emailed to permissionrequest@cengage.com

Articles in Greenhaven Press anthologies are often edited for length to meet page requirements. In addition, original titles of these works are changed to clearly present the main thesis and to explicitly indicate the author's opinion. Every effort is made to ensure that Greenhaven Press accurately reflects the original intent of the authors. Every effort has been made to trace the owners of copyrighted material.

Cover image: Ryan McVay/Getty Images

LIBRARY OF CONGRESS CATALOGING-IN-PUBLICATION DATA

Hamilton, Jill.
The music industry / Jill Hamilton, book editor.
  p. cm. -- (Introducing issues with opposing viewpoints)
 Includes bibliographical references and index.
 ISBN 978-0-7377-4339-5 (hardcover)
 1. Music trade--Juvenile literature. 2. Sound recording industry--Juvenile literature.
I. Title.
 ML3790.H329 2009
 338.4'7780973--dc22

                                                                    2009002467

Printed in the United States of America
1 2 3 4 5 6 7 13 12 11 10 09

Contents

Chapter 3: What Should the Rules Be for Downloading Music and Paying Artists?

Foreword

Indulging in a wide spectrum of ideas, beliefs, and perspectives is a critical cornerstone of democracy. After all, it is often debates over differences of opinion, such as whether to legalize abortion, how to treat prisoners, or when to enact the death penalty, that shape our society and drive it forward. Such diversity of thought is frequently regarded as the hallmark of a healthy and civilized culture. As the Reverend Clifford Schutjer of the First Congregational Church in Mansfield, Ohio, declared in a 2001 sermon, "Surrounding oneself with only like-minded people, restricting what we listen to or read only to what we find agreeable is irresponsible. Refusing to entertain doubts once we make up our minds is a subtle but deadly form of arrogance." With this advice in mind, Introducing Issues with Opposing Viewpoints books aim to open readers' minds to the critically divergent views that comprise our world's most important debates.

Introducing Issues with Opposing Viewpoints simplifies for students the enormous and often overwhelming mass of material now available via print and electronic media. Collected in every volume is an array of opinions that captures the essence of a particular controversy or topic. Introducing Issues with Opposing Viewpoints books embody the spirit of nineteenth-century journalist Charles A. Dana's axiom: "Fight for your opinions, but do not believe that they contain the whole truth, or the only truth." Absorbing such contrasting opinions teaches students to analyze the strength of an argument and compare it to its opposition. From this process readers can inform and strengthen their own opinions, or be exposed to new information that will change their minds. Introducing Issues with Opposing Viewpoints is a mosaic of different voices. The authors are statesmen, pundits, academics, journalists, corporations, and ordinary people who have felt compelled to share their experiences and ideas in a public forum. Their words have been collected from newspapers, journals, books, speeches, interviews, and the Internet, the fastest growing body of opinionated material in the world.

Introducing Issues with Opposing Viewpoints shares many of the well-known features of its critically acclaimed parent series, Opposing Viewpoints. The articles are presented in a pro/con format, allowing readers to absorb divergent perspectives side by side. Active reading questions preface each viewpoint, requiring the student to approach the material thoughtfully and carefully. Useful charts, graphs, and cartoons supplement each article. A thorough introduction provides readers with crucial background on an issue. An annotated bibliography points the reader toward articles, books, and Web sites that contain additional information on the topic. An appendix of organizations to contact contains a wide variety of charities, nonprofit organizations, political groups, and private enterprises that each hold a position on the issue at hand. Finally, a comprehensive index allows readers to locate content quickly and efficiently.

Introducing Issues with Opposing Viewpoints is also significantly different from Opposing Viewpoints. As the series title implies, its presentation will help introduce students to the concept of opposing viewpoints and learn to use this material to aid in critical writing and debate. The series' four-color, accessible format makes the books attractive and inviting to readers of all levels. In addition, each viewpoint has been carefully edited to maximize a reader's understanding of the content. Short but thorough viewpoints capture the essence of an argument. A substantial, thought-provoking essay question placed at the end of each viewpoint asks the student to further investigate the issues raised in the viewpoint, compare and contrast two authors' arguments, or consider how one might go about forming an opinion on the topic at hand. Each viewpoint contains sidebars that include at-a-glance information and handy statistics. A Facts About section located in the back of the book further supplies students with relevant facts and figures.

Following in the tradition of the Opposing Viewpoints series, Greenhaven Press continues to provide readers with invaluable exposure to the controversial issues that shape our world. As John Stuart Mill once wrote: "The only way in which a human being can make some approach to knowing the whole of a subject is by hearing what can be said about it by persons of every variety of opinion and studying all modes in which it can be looked at by every character of mind. No wise man ever acquired his wisdom in any mode but this." It is to this principle that Introducing Issues with Opposing Viewpoints books are dedicated.

Introduction

"All our business practices need to change."

—An unnamed record company CEO,
quoted in *U.S. News & World Report*

The first decade of the twenty-first century has been a tumultuous time for the music industry. A rash of technological developments, including file sharing, satellite radio, and social networks, are irrevocably changing the face of the industry. The industry is struggling with what its role in the future will be—or even if it will continue to exist at all.

Such upheaval is new for the industry, which had enjoyed a largely trouble-free existence for over a hundred years. Since the late 1800s, when the general public started buying recorded music for entertainment, the music industry has been there to provide it—and profit from it. The last half of the twentieth century was the heyday for the record industry. Youth culture exploded, and with it came massive record sales, huge concert tours, and plenty of money to be made. Consumers spent enough money on music to fund a slew of high-paying music-related jobs, including those for producers, recording studio engineers, entertainment lawyers, album art designers, and publicists.

Now the entire music industry is in a flux. Technology has changed how music is delivered, how people listen to it, and how it is promoted. One huge factor has been the advent of digital downloading. In one way this could be a boon for record companies—after all, more digital downloads means less of the manufacturing costs associated with producing CDs. But record companies seem flummoxed by not having a physical product to sell and have not yet found a satisfactory new business model. Record companies have been slow to respond to the new business realities and have not yet taken a leadership role in developing and using new technologies.

Illegal downloading is a challenging issue as well. File sharing and P2P (peer-to-peer) technology has made it easier than ever for people to find and trade music without ever paying anyone. It is not just record companies that are concerned—many artists and other workers in the music industry are worried about illegal downloading because it affects their bottom line as well. The music industry is responding to illegal downloading in various ways. Record companies are focusing most of their efforts on fighting illegal downloading through lawsuits and public information campaigns. But the band Radiohead tried another tactic and offered downloads of their record *In Rainbows* in a pay-what-you-want model. Other bands are offering their music online for free in hopes that they will stir up enough interest to make money through touring and sales of promotional items.

The big question is whether, with so much music available for free, music will become so devalued that people will not pay for it. So far, the answer has been no. Although free illegal downloads are readily available, there is still a huge population of people willing to pay for music downloads when doing so is easy and relatively inexpensive. The huge success of Apple's iTunes is an indication of that. According to *Wired*, iTunes has sold more than 7 billion songs and approximately 70 percent of all digital music sold worldwide.

Social networking sites like MySpace and video sites like YouTube have changed the way consumers discover music and how bands promote themselves. Just ten years ago the only ways for bands to get wide attention were through constant touring, a record company deal, or securing broad, positive media coverage. Now, with a few dollars and a camera, a band can put a video on YouTube and, within days, have a worldwide viral hit. Social networking sites can also help bands who play obscure or specialized kinds of music to connect with like-minded potential fans quickly and easily. And instead of needing to hire a publicist to send press releases to radio stations and newspapers, bands can make their own promotional materials and have them online and available to a nationwide audience in a rapid time frame.

Radio has also undergone radical changes. Listeners not only have AM and FM to choose from, but also satellite radio, Internet radio, and online Web sites like Pandora that offer customized radio stations based on a listener's individual musical taste. These developments change the way music is promoted to listeners. In the past if certain influential radio stations played a song enough times, it would generally become popular. In the 1950s payola (paying a radio station to play a certain song) was scandalous not only because it was illegal, but because it worked. Now payola probably would not have the same effect. There are so many stations that a single one no longer wields the same power. The Top 40 stations of an earlier time are being replaced by increasingly specialized stations. XM Satellite Radio for example, does not have just one rock radio station, but sixteen, including one devoted entirely to the music of Led Zeppelin.

All of these changes make for an unpredictable future for the music industry. In *Introducing Issues with Opposing Viewpoints: The Music Industry*, the authors offer their views on the big issues facing the industry today, including illegal downloading, whether or not social networking sitcs should pay royalties, and whether or not CDs are dead. The way in which these debates are eventually resolved will transform the music industry and shape its future for companies, artists, and consumers.

Chapter 1

How Healthy Is the Music Industry?

The music industry has gone through some changes in recent years, but fans still pack big venues to see their favorite musicians.

Record Labels Are Becoming Irrelevant

Ian Bezek

"In an age when music is widely available, the traditional model for a record label doesn't work."

In the following essay Ian Bezek criticizes record labels for not adjusting to new trends in how people obtain and listen to music. He cites cases in which labels have sued users of music downloading sites and pulled popular videos from YouTube. Such tactics are not only ineffectual, the author argues, but they also create a bad relationship between the label and the customer. Bezek suggests that record companies would be better off selling music cheaply or even giving it away and earning revenue from live shows and merchandise sales. Bezek wrote this article while studying economics at Colorado State University.

AS YOU READ, CONSIDER THE FOLLOWING QUESTIONS:

1. What does the author describe as "revolutionary new developments in music"?
2. According to the author, in what way did record labels treat customers poorly when CDs were introduced?
3. The author suggests that record companies sell "the experience" of music. How does he propose that they do that?

American record labels seem to think we're still living in the 1970s. Instead of modernizing with our new technology, they have remained fixed in their stale old business plan.

Despite revolutionary new developments in music such as the Internet and iPods, record labels insist on selling music by the album, gouging a listener for $15 to buy a CD with only two or three good songs.

The labels have a long history of treating their customers poorly. After the switch from vinyl to compact discs, the labels jacked up the price of music despite the fact that CDs were far cheaper to manufacture.

The music industry has shown even poorer judgment recently, though. Their decision to sue users of Napster and its descendants was entirely misguided. Their protection schemes on music that is legitimately purchased from places like iTunes also make no sense.

People Use New Ways to Discover Music

In an age when music is widely available, the traditional model for a record label doesn't work. Record labels traditionally would bribe radio stations to play their new songs and then promote their albums on the basis of those radio hits.

I don't know about you, but I don't rely on the radio to find new music anymore. Much of today's good music is found far beyond the narrow walls of traditional commercial radio, yet record labels attack the other outlets of finding new music.

For example, when Linkin Park came out with a new single last year, their record label, Warner Music, repeatedly forced YouTube to take down the music video for it. Warner should have considered themselves blessed that people were eager to watch their band perform; instead they limited the spread of a new song and angered fans.

The future of music is not going to be found in selling CDs that cost a dime each to produce at exorbitant prices.

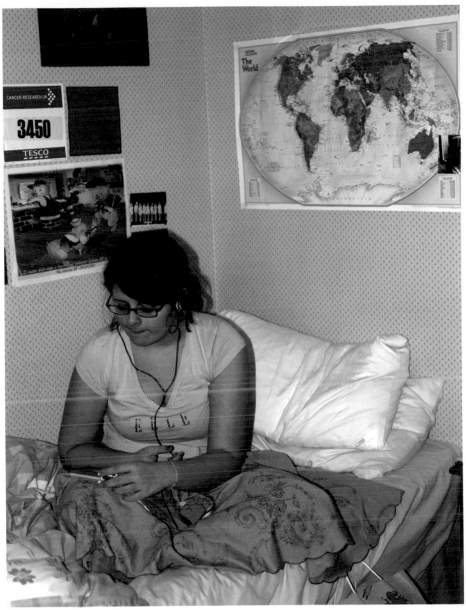

A teenager listens to music on her iPod. The Internet for music downloads and the iPod are making traditional record labels obsolete, says the author.

The record labels can try to stop this if they want—Sony attached a virus to many of their CDs last year that infected their customers' computers, including mine. Despite becoming angry with them, I was not deterred from making digital copies of my music to various portable devices I own.

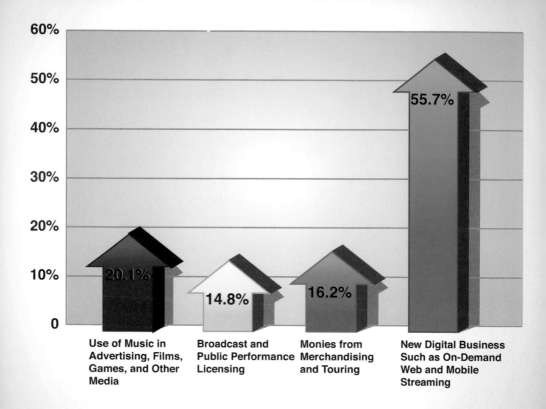

Increase in UK Record Label Revenues from Sources Other than Direct Music Sales, 2007

- Use of Music in Advertising, Films, Games, and Other Media: 20.1%
- Broadcast and Public Performance Licensing: 14.8%
- Monies from Merchandising and Touring: 16.2%
- New Digital Business Such as On-Demand Web and Mobile Streaming: 55.7%

Taken from: Mark Hefflinger, "Report: Label Revenue Outside Direct Music Sales Up 14%," Digital Media Wire, July 1, 2008.

Sell "the Experience" of Music

Music is all about the experience, and if the popularity of bands on MySpace shows anything, music is as popular as it has ever been. The record labels need to promote the experience, via tours and merchandise, rather than the sale of CDs we don't want.

Just last week, I paid $35 to see some bands I like down in Denver, and purchased an overpriced band shirt as well. I was willing to do this because I went for the experience of seeing the bands.

It is very easy to get music for free or almost free off the Internet or from sharing discs with a friend. On the other hand, it is impossible to download the experience of seeing a live concert.

Record labels should be selling music very cheaply, or even giving it away, to promote their artists. As Chris Anderson describes in his book "The Long Tail," Reprise Records, for instance, allowed songs from an upcoming My Chemical Romance album to be freely leaked around the Internet.

Much to their surprise, a song that they had low expectations for became highly popular across the illegal download sites. Reprise trusted the fans and promoted that song, "Helena," which became a smash hit propelling the band to super stardom. Since then My Chemical Romance has generated vast income from its concerts.

CD sales have fallen off a cliff. It's time for the music industry to boldly break with the past, stop angering its customers, and promote the experience of music—which unlike albums—cannot be pirated.

EVALUATING THE AUTHOR'S ARGUMENTS:

The author uses a lot of short, sometimes personal anecdotes to further his argument. Is this an effective technique? How do you think a college student might respond to this essay? Do you think an adult would have a different response?

Record Labels Are More Necessary than Ever

Paul Sloan

"Most acts still need a big machine behind them, which for now means the labels."

In the following article author Paul Sloan argues that in today's music market, record labels are still a necessity. To make his case, he follows the release of Matchbox Twenty's album *Exile on Mainstream*. He contacted the band's label, Atlantic Records, and found that the company was armed with a forty-one-page marketing plan dedicated to promoting the band. Such marketing expertise facilitates extra publicity for the band, including TV appearances and special deals with iTunes, YouTube, and VH1 .com. Even though the music industry has changed, Sloan argues, bands still need that kind of large-scale publicity machine behind them to break through the clutter. Sloan is a senior writer for *Fortune* magazine.

AS YOU READ, CONSIDER THE FOLLOWING QUESTIONS:

1. Due to the record company's various marketing plans, what were some of the many versions of Matchbox Twenty's album made available?

2. Name three promotional techniques Atlantic Records used to promote Matchbox Twenty's record *Exile on Mainstream.*
3. The Internet helps bands get music out more easily, but, according to the author, there is a drawback. What is it?

(*Fortune*)—In the music business, promotion is paramount—and that's why the bracelets are such a great idea.

Warner Music (Charts) and AT&T (Charts, Fortune 500) Mobility threw a swank, invite-only bash at a San Francisco nightspot recently, featuring a concert by the multi-platinum band Matchbox Twenty. Attendees received a black rubber bracelet that doubles as a USB device. Plug it in your computer and, voila, you get the band's latest album, *Exile on Mainstream*, plus a video and other digital goodies. Pretty cool.

The bracelet itself, which includes 17 songs, plus video interviews and a digital booklet with album art, is now on sale for about $35 at Best Buy (Charts, Fortune 500) and other stores. It isn't about to resurrect the ailing music industry. But it does show the efforts that the labels are undertaking to get music out in this entirely disruptive digital age.

It's easy to think that these days musicians can go it alone, and the evidence seems ample. British rockers Radiohead recently eschewed the major labels and released their latest album, *In Rainbows*, on its Website, letting fans pay what they want to download it. Trent Reznor of Nine Inch Nails said he would follow suit. And Madonna just jumped from Warner Music after snagging a lucrative deal with Live Nation, a company that puts on concerts.

Big Week Ahead for the Giants of Media

So who needs the labels? Well, major acts like Matchbox Twenty, for starters; and, for that matter, most any band that aspires to such heights.

Matchbox Twenty, which is fronted by Rob Thomas, has been with Warner Music Group's Atlantic Records for ten years. The band gets tons of radio play and has sold some 28 million albums. When I asked Livia Tortella, Atlantic's general manager and executive vice president of marketing and creative media, how her team

Forecast of Compact Discs Versus Digital Recorded Music Sales, 2006

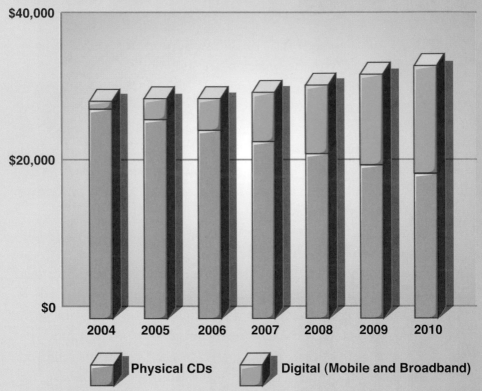

Millions of U.S. Dollars

Taken from: Anton Shilov, "Digital Music Market to Reach $14.9 Billion by 2010," Xbit Laboratories, November 24, 2006.

is promoting *Exile on Mainstream*, she shot over a 41-page, "phase I" marketing plan.

It's packed with info that would have been found on such a plan a decade ago—dates on Jay Leno and elsewhere, scheduled radio interviews and so on—but it also sheds light on the complexity of today's chaotic marketplace.

Consider how Atlantic released the album—rather, all 11 versions of it, if you include the bracelet. Fans who pre-ordered the entire album on Apple's (Charts, Fortune 500) iTunes got the single, "How Far We've Come," at the time of purchase, plus a bonus track. There were bundled offerings on iTunes that included extra songs if you chose the non a la carte option. Wal-Mart (Charts, Fortune 500) shoppers got exclusive video. A deal with Viacom's (Charts, Fortune 500) VH1.com gave that channel an exclusive stream of the album a week prior to the in-store release date. And this is just a sampling.

Atlantic also landed a featured spot for the band's video on Google's (Charts, Fortune 500) YouTube, and it premiered some content on News Corp's (Charts, Fortune 500) MySpace. Then there are mobile deals, such as the one with AT&T Mobility, where customers had access to exclusive live audio and streaming video as part of the launch of its over-the-air download store. Matchbox Twenty was featured on the screen that mobile users first see when hunting for music.

Madonna Picks Live Nation over Warner Bros.

"That is as exciting as getting an MTV spin," says Tortella. And when Matchbox Twenty has news it wants to get out—an upcoming TV appearance, for example—the label blasts text messages to fans. "The scope of what we're doing is so much more diverse than it was even two years ago," says Tortella. "There are a lot of people touching this act, and we're hitting fans on all fronts."

Viewed this way, the opportunities for artists bigger and better than ever before. Yet for as much as the Internet helps bands get

FAST FACT

It is difficult to determine exactly how many record labels there are, but estimates range from twenty-five hundred to thirty-eight hundred worldwide.

music out, in some ways it also makes it harder to get noticed—at least on a grand scale. That's why most acts still need a big machine behind them, which for now means the labels.

"How else do you break through all the noise?" says Donald Passman, author of "All You Need to Know About the Music

Established bands like Matchbox Twenty, above, are marketing their music through the Internet and concerts but still need their record company's marketing power, argues this viewpoint's author.

Business," and Radiohead's attorney. Even Radiohead, held out in the press as the rebels of the industry, is negotiating to once again sign with a label.

Of course, the trick for the labels is to figure out how to make more money off this ever-more laborious process of distributing and marketing bands. CD sales, still the bulk of the business for now, continue to slide, and no one has figured out how to replace that once-lucrative cash machine.

This is no easy task, and the transition is proving painful for investors. Warner Music Group's stock, for example, is trading around $9, down from about $25 just six months ago.

But for music lovers, the digital age is proving anything but painful. Who, after all, would want to return to a world with only CDs? I, for one, am hoping for more USB bracelets.

EVALUATING THE AUTHOR'S ARGUMENTS:

The author leads with an anecdote about Matchbox Twenty and then extends it by examining the band's career from a wider angle, including interviews with industry figures. How do you think this technique compares with the one used in the previous viewpoint, which relied heavily on personal observations?

The CD Is Dead

Aidin Vaziri

"Suddenly the thought of owning an awkward polycarbonate plastic-coated disc that holds only an hour of tunes by just one artist seems positively prehistoric."

The time has come for CDs to fade into history, argues Aidin Vaziri in the following article. Vaziri starts with a brief litany of complaints about CDs, including their penchant for skipping and their non-ergonomic jewel cases. According to the author, when there is such a plethora of other, cheaper and easier methods of listening to music, there is no reason to cling to outmoded CDs. To further his point, he lists ten alternatives to the rapidly disappearing discs, including seeing live music and listening to online radio and MP3 blogs. Vaziri is pop music critic for the *San Francisco Chronicle*.

AS YOU READ, CONSIDER THE FOLLOWING QUESTIONS:

1. The author recommends three online radio stations. What are they?
2. What technology, according to the author, is reportedly responsible for one-third of the Web's traffic?
3. Most of the author's suggestions for a CD-free existence involve new technology. Name one that uses old technology.

They're overpriced, ugly and don't even make good rearview mirror ornaments. Now that we know they are also potentially poisonous to personal computers, thanks to Sony BMG's rogue copy-protection technology [some copy-protection software on Sony discs allowed easy access for virus writers], there's really no reason to buy another compact disc ever again.

With sleek iPods rapidly becoming the hi-fi system of choice, satellite radio offering hundreds of specialty stations, and the Internet overflowing with all kinds of free and cheap legal digital music, suddenly the thought of owning an awkward polycarbonate plastic-coated disc that holds only an hour of tunes by just one artist seems positively prehistoric—even if it comes with a hastily produced "bonus" DVD.

It's clearly time to move on. Think about it: No more nails-on-chalkboard-style skipping. No more secret tracks that scare the stuffing out of you 15 minutes after you think an album has stopped playing. No more fumbling around with those impossible-to-unwrap jewel cases. It was fun while it lasted. The music industry has declared war on its customers. Now it's time to fight back. Below we explain the 10 best ways to get the most out of the next musical revolution.

Beyond CDs

1. *MP3 blogs*: The Internet isn't just a great place to find amateur porn and clips of fat kids acting out scenes from "The Phantom Menace." It's actually an incredible resource for discovering new music and the best sites to do that at the moment are MP3 blogs such as The Hype Machine (hype.non-standard.net) and Largehearted Boy (blog. largeheartedboy.com), which offer daily, no-nonsense links to free music available online. Meanwhile, personal blogs such as Stereogum (www.stereogum.com), Sixeyes (sixeyes.blogspot.com) and Said the Gramophone (www.saidthegramophone.com) hand out iPod-friendly tunes along with smartly written previews. For those with a couple of hours, weeks or months to kill, a staggering list of MP3 blogs is available at the Tofu Hut (tofuhut.blogspot.com).

2. *Online radio*: While terrestrial radio stations choke on corporate policies, automated playlists and buzz-killing commercial breaks, online radio stations are becoming a safe haven for anyone who just wants to hear some good music. One of the best is Los Angeles–based public radio station KCRW (www.kcrw.com). Its daily "Morning

Becomes Eclectic" program, hosted by Nic Harcourt, never ceases to amaze, mixing everything from indie rock and world beat to classical and jazz. Where else can you hear the Arctic Monkeys, Johnny Cash and Bebel Gilberto back to back? Another great station, Cincinnati's WOXY FM (www.woxy.com), set up shop on the Internet after it was bumped off the air. Now it reaches a worldwide audience with an adventurous mix of alternative rock. San Francisco's contribution to the online radio market is SOMA FM (www.somafm.com), a listener-supported portal providing eight channels of mostly electronic-based music.

FAST FACT

The average cost for a physical CD is $15.98. The average cost for a downloaded album is $10.00.

3. *Digital music services.* Owning music is so last century. With everyone bent on cutting the clutter, it makes sense to sign up with a digital music service that puts a head-spinning, commitment-free music library at your disposal. Rhapsody (www.rhapsody.com) and Napster (www.napster.com)—formerly an illegal peer-to-peer service—are the big ones, giving subscribers more than a million songs to choose from and providing interactive radio for those who just can't decide what they want to hear. They both tend to lean heavily toward more mainstream releases, but neither allows much room for the kind of boredom that sets in after listening to your Billy Idol greatest hits CD for the 789th time.

4. *MySpace music.* MySpace.com is an enormous online social networking site that was recently purchased by Rupert Murdoch's News Corp. for $580 million. It counts more than 37 million members, most of them falling into the coveted teen demographic. So it only makes sense that the place is simply bursting with music. Both upcoming acts and major labels use it as a way to reach new audiences, with artists like Nine Inch Nails, Madonna, Black Eyed Peas, Neil Diamond and R.E.M. even going so far as to put up exclusive previews of their albums before they hit the streets. For the more adventurous, there are more than 55,000 unsigned bands of varying quality, just begging for anyone to listen. You have to figure anything's got to be better than the new Scott Stapp album.

5. *Satellite radio*: Howard Stern is moving to Sirius (www.sirius .com). Mercedes-Benz plans to make the satellite radio service a standard feature in its luxury sedans. Snoop Dogg appears in TV spots for XM (www.xmradio.com), while the company has wired JetBlue planes with more than 100 channels of its programming. We don't know much about the stock market, but it seems like a

New music technologies like the iPod, the Internet, and satellite radio have made the venerable CD a thing of the past, says the author.

good idea to invest both money and time in what has to be one of the fastest growing entertainment services in the world. Offering more variety than even a 60-gig iPod and more unpredictability than the wildest shuffle imaginable, these subscription-based services are simply a must-have for anyone with a daily commute of more than five minutes.

6. *iTunes Music Store*: This is the obvious one. Despite restrictive file formats that allow only a limited number of transfers for purchased MP3s, there's a good reason why it is the most popular download service by a mile. With simple across-the-board pricing and lots of exclusive content, the Apple Music Store is the example nearly every new music service will follow from here on out.

7. *Hit the clubs*: The best way to experience music, of course, is to ditch the fancy gadgets and go straight to the source. In the Bay Area, we're fortunate to have an abundance of excellent live music venues that cater to nearly every whim. Whether it's the Lovemakers at the Fillmore, Armand Van Helden at 1015 Folsom or Zion I at the Independent, there's enough going on on any given night to prevent anyone from missing those old CDs.

8. *BitTorrent*: People used to exchange live Grateful Dead and Bob Dylan bootlegs on crummy tapes by seeking out fellow traders through cheaply produced fanzines that came out once every four years. Now they just point-and-click toward the legally nebulous BitTorrent (www.bittorrent.com), a computer program that allows users to share huge files over the Internet. The exchange of torrents, which can contain anything from music and software to the latest "Star Wars" movie six hours before its official release, is said to be responsible for one-third of the Web's traffic. The entire recording of Dave Matthews Band "Live at Golden Gate Park" on crystal-clear digital audio? No problem. The latest Coldplay concert video that Chris Martin hasn't even seen yet? There it is. The Strokes' latest album four months before it hits stores? Better call your attorney.

9. *Amazon.com free music downloads*: To entice people to buy new music, Amazon has an incredible free music downloads page loaded with MP3s from new and old releases spanning practically every genre imaginable. There is so much good stuff available from the likes of

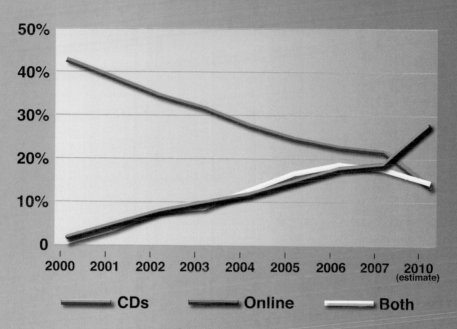

Trends in Music Media Purchases

CDs — Online — Both

Taken from. Bridge Ratings. "Music Consumption Study," June 20, 2007.

the Arcade Fire, Alison Krauss and Beck, you might be forgiven for never getting around to actually purchasing anything.

10. *Rock it old school*: Let's be honest, somehow R.E.M. never sounded better than when it was blaring out of the college dorm room boom box with all that tape hiss in the background. Led Zeppelin's "Black Dog" doesn't make nearly as much sense as digital ones-and-zeros as it does on a slab of dusty, crackling vinyl. And the 7-inch single of Blondie's "Dreaming" still sends shivers down the spine.

All the classic albums made before the CD revolution hit in 1982—some might argue the only albums anyone really needs—are abundantly available in vinyl form, most for less than the price of one lousy Black Eyed Peas song on iTunes. Try garage sales, street corners, the bottom shelves at [California-based independent music store] Amoeba, or, better yet, buy up entire lots of records and tapes on eBay. Fortunately, there's a booming market for retro-themed record players in stores like Restoration Hardware and Target, while once sleek Walkman cassette players are practically spilling off the electronics shelves and into the bric-a-brac aisles at Goodwill stores everywhere. Going back to basics has never made more sense.

EVALUATING THE AUTHOR'S ARGUMENTS:

The author does not spend much space arguing that CDs are becoming extinct and instead focuses on options beyond CDs. In what way might this make for a stronger case than if he had spent several paragraphs outlining more reasons why CDs were no longer viable?

Viewpoint
4

The CD Is Still Viable

Daniel Gross

In the following viewpoint author Daniel Gross reacts to the many articles that have been written saying that the CD is dead. He argues that, although it is true CD sales are declining, there are still a lot of CDs being sold and notes that CDs are the main way people buy music. The successful CD sellers of the future will be businesses that can figure out the right way to market CDs. He uses Amazon as an example of a business selling CDs the right way, pointing out that their low prices and central warehouses help keep customers happy and costs low. Gross is the "Moneybox" columnist for *Slate* and the business columnist for *Newsweek*.

> "The CD is dead! *Except, it's not.*"

AS YOU READ, CONSIDER THE FOLLOWING QUESTIONS:
1. How much does Gross say CD sales were down in the first quarter of 2007?
2. What portion of all music sold is in the form of CDs, according to the author?
3. What other industry does the author compare music retailers and manufacturers to?

Daniel Gross, "The CD Is Dead! Long Live the CD!" *Slate*, March 27, 2007. © Washington Post. Newsweek Interactive Co., LLC.

ozart wrote only one *Requiem,* but in recent years, music journalists have written about 80 requiems for the compact disc, mostly in the key of boo-hoo major. Data from the Recording Industry Association of America show that between 2000 and 2005, the number of CDs shipped fell 25 percent to 705.4 million, while their value slipped 20 percent, from $13.2 billion to $10.5 billion. During the first six months of 2006, CD sales dropped 14 percent more. And as Ethan Smith wrote in the *Wall Street Journal* last week [March 2007], CD sales are down another 20 percent in the first quarter of 2007. On Monday, Jeff Leeds, writing in the *New York Times,* penned an obituary for the CD, which has been driven into oblivion by consumers' preference for digital singles over albums. Last year [2006], hundreds of music stores closed, among them the 89 outlets of the greatly missed Tower Records.

Conclusion: *The CD is dead!*

Not Dead Yet

Except, it's not. Last Sunday, Paul de Barros of the *Seattle Times* chronicled the growth of Silver Platters, a local chain of CD stores that just took over an old Tower Records space. Meanwhile, savvy new-era businesses are jumping into the CD business. The same day Smith's piece appeared in the *Journal,* Starbucks announced its record label would issue its first CD this summer, from Paul McCartney. Earlier this month, Amazon launched a classical music retail outlet, capitalizing on the genre's impressive 2006 comeback, which was driven by massive CD sales from the unholy trinity of cheesy, nonclassical classical artists: Andrea Bocelli, Josh Groban, and Il Divo.

> **FAST FACT**
>
> Some of the reasons people list for purchasing CDs include: getting the physical CD, cover art, and case; wanting to support the band; and feeling that the music is less likely to get lost or deleted on a CD.

Clearly, it's trickier than ever to make, market, and sell CDs. It's an industry in crisis. But CDs are still a significant business. All the kids, and many adults, have iPods.

A Gradual Decline in CD Sales

This chart shows manufacturers' unit shipments and retail dollar value of CDs (in millions, net, after returns).

	Units Shipped	Dollar Value
1997	753.1	$9,915.1
1998	847.0	$11,416.0
1999	938.9	$12,816.3
2000	942.5	$13,214.5
2001	881.9	$12,909.4
2002	803.3	$12,044.1
2003	746.0	$11,232.9
2004	767.0	$11,446.5
2005	705.4	$10,520.2
2006	619.7	$9,372.6
2007	511.1	$7,452.3

Taken from: RIAA. www.riaa.com/keystatistics.php, 2008.

But plenty of baby boomers still buy the shiny discs; CDs account for three-quarters of all music sold.

What we are witnessing is not so much the imminent death of CDs but the death of the old methods of selling CDs. It's still possible to make money in the CD business—any business with more than $7 billion in retail sales should allow someone, somewhere, to make a profit. The incumbents are getting killed, but upstarts are thriving, using different methods.

Legacy music retailers and manufacturers now face many of the same difficulties as American auto companies. They built a business infrastructure—national chains, huge outlets in high-profile locations,

Large music retailers have had a difficult time in the CD retail business because file sharing and iTunes make purchasing music cheaper.

layers of management—predicated on selling massive and growing quantities of CDs for $15.99 and up. Like the American automakers, they found that new competition—from iTunes, file-sharing, and online retailers—severely cut into their margins, their market share, and their pricing power. In such an environment, companies with significant capital invested in stores and substantial overhead costs get destroyed. And as they fall, they do so loudly, inspiring widespread pessimism.

New Ways of Doing Business

Yet the new rules open opportunities for upstarts who approach the business of making and marketing CDs in a fundamentally different way. Unlike fallen chains such as Tower, boutiques such as Silver Platters and Rasputin in San Francisco don't spend on expensive national advertising. They're more like art-house theaters. Since they cater more to music aficionados than to the masses who used to flood into HMV for the latest Mariah Carey CD, the demise of the block-buster CD doesn't put a crimp in their sales.

In the age of file-sharing and iTunes, people simply aren't willing to pay $16 for a collection of songs they may not want. That proved to be fatal for Tower Records. But for Amazon.com, such price pressure doesn't really matter. The company has built up a commercial infrastructure that enables it to sell and deliver all sorts of cheap objects, from books to toys. Blogger Barry Ritholtz noted in January that most of the top-selling CDs at Amazon.com sell for *less than $10*. For Amazon, which already has huge investments in warehouses, software, and its Web site, carving out some extra space for classical CDs doesn't require a huge incremental investment. What's more, since its inception, the store has been designed to run on very low margins.

In the case of Starbucks, the economics of selling CDs are even more compelling. With its 14,000-odd outlets, the company already has a massive, highly profitable retail channel that generates immense foot traffic daily. Each store is conveniently outfitted with counters, which are ideal for stocking a variety of noncoffee products that have mass appeal: chocolates, books, and CDs. Both Barnes & Noble and Borders may be having a difficult time making money selling wide selections of books in huge retail spaces. But when Starbucks decides to stock a single book, say Mitch Albom's *For One More Day* or Ishmael Beah's *A Long Way Gone*, it can easily turn a profit on every sale. Starbucks found the same sort of success with the Ray Charles album *Genius Loves Company* in 2004. Starbucks has also invested in building its Hear Music concept, where customers can buy coffee, buy CDs, or download music, into a small chain.

Is the CD dying as a commercial product? Sure. But it's got a lot of dying left to do. And in the meantime, there's still money to be made selling discs loaded with the music of Josh Groban, Alban Berg, and Rod Stewart.

EVALUATING THE AUTHOR'S ARGUMENTS:

What are the most convincing arguments the author makes to show that CDs are not a dead format?

Big Box Stores Are Changing Consumer Tastes

Ethan Smith

"Today, many music industry executives agree, the big boxes have become the new tastemakers."

In the following article Ethan Smith notes the ways that big box stores—that is, large general merchandising chains like Wal-Mart, Target, and Best Buy—are changing the kinds of music that are available to consumers. Unlike a specialty record store that seeks to provide a wide variety of choices to music buyers, big box stores offer customers only the most popular albums. This practice makes it more difficult for more specialty genres to get shelf space, and even a perennially popular band like The Beatles may only have one or two records on the shelf. Furthermore, some retailers demand clean versions of albums, in which all material they deem to be offensive is deleted or censored. Smith writes about the music industry for the *Wall Street Journal*.

AS YOU READ, CONSIDER THE FOLLOWING QUESTIONS:
1. Why is Green Day's album *American Idiot* not sold in Wal-Mart stores?

Ethan Smith, "Can Music Survive Inside the Big Box?" *The Wall Street Journal,* April 27, 2007. Reprinted with permission of *The Wall Street Journal.*

2. According to the article, how many CD titles does a typical Best Buy stock?
3. Name three types of music that have trouble getting shelf space in a big box store, according to the author.

When Wal-Mart Stores Inc. informed record labels it was looking for CDs to include in a promotion of Jewish music last year [2006], executives at Naxos of America Inc. leapt at the chance to get some of their ethnic recordings onto the shelves of the big-box retailer.

But within months of shipping thousands of CDs to Wal-Mart, the classical music distributor's loading docks were swamped with unsold copies of "Klezmer Concertos & Encores" and "Great Songs of the Yiddish Stage." Since they hadn't sold quickly enough to meet the retailing giant's standards, 80% of the CDs Naxos shipped to Wal-Mart were returned. Record stores typically return only 20%.

"In hindsight, if we'd thought about this a little more, we wouldn't have done it," says Naxos Chief Operating Officer Jim Selby. "Jewish classical music, going into a Wal-Mart store, it's pretty farfetched that we'd have 60% or 70% sell through." He adds, "It's niche-y music."

Music executives—and not just those who traffic in obscure genres—are in an increasing bind when it comes to selling their wares on CD. As dedicated music stores, including Tower Records, have closed up shop by the thousands, big, generalist chains like Wal-Mart, Target Corp. and Best Buy Co. have tightened their already firm grip on the sale of physical CDs. The chains order huge quantities of some titles, while other releases find it hard to get a foothold.

Big Box Stores Are Shaping Trends

In past decades, deejays and music critics helped shape musical trends. Today, many music industry executives agree, the big boxes have become the new tastemakers. Even as compact disc sales fall, their choices dictate which CDs are widely available on store shelves across the U.S. Big boxes are the industry's biggest distribution channel—and the rock, hip-hop, jazz and classical music titles they choose not to carry face drastically reduced chances of reaching mass audiences.

Thanks largely to aggressive pricing and advertising, big-box chains are now responsible in the U.S. for at least 65% of music sales (including online and physical recordings), according to estimates by distribution executives, up from 20% a decade ago. Where a store that depends on CDs for the bulk of its sales needs a profit margin of around 30%, big chains get by making just 14% on music, say label executives who handle distribution. One of these executives describes the shift as "a tidal wave." Despite the growth in online digital music sales, physical CDs still are the core of the recording industry, accounting for about 85% of music sales.

Big-box chains say they're trying to give customers what they want. "We also are making changes to the CD selections in our stores to reflect customer preferences in each market," says a Wal-Mart spokeswoman.

But some labels worry that the big boxes are becoming even more restrictive in what they carry. That's partly because, with CD sales falling steeply, the discs aren't as hot as other products the stores sell. Also in the wake of the Don Imus controversy [racist comments aired by the controversial radio personality], the debate over the lyrical content of rap, rock and pop has flared up again. Oprah Winfrey recently has focused on rap lyrics on her talk show.

Stores Demand "Clean" Versions of Albums

Wal-Mart, for example, has long refused to carry any album bearing a "parental advisory" label warning of lyrics that are potentially inappropriate for minors. As a result, major record labels typically create sanitized versions of albums for sale there and at other sensitive retailers. People in the music industry, however, say some hip hop and rock albums can be difficult to sell to the big chain—even if the releases lack controversial content. "Even Target's getting more difficult," says Jeff Rabhan, a talent manager who has pop and hip hop

Big box stores like Wal-Mart offer only the most popular-selling CDs, which makes it difficult for new and specialty bands to get shelf space and thus increased sales.

clients. "Especially with everything that's going on right now with Imus and Oprah, it is becoming increasingly difficult to get hip hop records prominently displayed and even in some cases stocked," Mr. Rabhan adds.

Wal-Mart's stores don't sell a number of prominent, popular releases, including the punk band Green Day's best-selling album "American Idiot," the critically acclaimed alternative rock band The Strokes' "First Impressions of Earth," and rapper Mos Def's "Black on Both Sides." A Wal-Mart spokeswoman says these releases aren't carried because edited versions aren't available.

The chains tend to emphasize fast-selling hits that move tens of thousands of units a week. A typical Best Buy stocks 8,000 to 20,000 different music CD titles, according to Gary Arnold, the chain's senior vice president for entertainment. Some chains carry even fewer titles. By contrast, the biggest of the defunct Tower's 89 locations carried more than 100,000 titles. (Tower still has some online operations.)

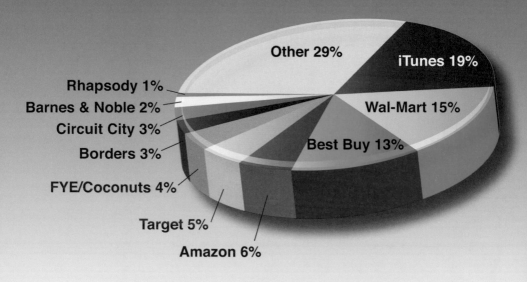

The Top Ten Music Retailers

Other 29%

iTunes 19%

Rhapsody 1%

Barnes & Noble 2%

Circuit City 3%

Borders 3%

Wal-Mart 15%

Best Buy 13%

FYE/Coconuts 4%

Target 5%

Amazon 6%

Taken from: The NPD Group, "NPD Music Watch Survey," February 2008.

It's not just classical music and jazz that have trouble making it into the big boxes. Up-and-coming pop, rock or hip hop acts are unlikely to be welcome until they are proven sellers. And back catalog titles are also feeling the squeeze; even the Beatles are frequently represented in big chain outlets by just one or two albums. That means there are fewer places than ever to buy any CDs but the newest, most heavily promoted titles.

Big Box Stores May Reduce CD Stock

What's more, as CD sales have slipped—sales have plunged 20% so far this year—big chains are starting to de-emphasize them. Best Buy's Mr. Arnold says his chain has reduced the square footage allotted to CDs across the chain over the past year, though the size of the reduction varies by store. "Certain businesses are starting to flourish at the expense of others," says Mr. Arnold. "Right now the hottest categories in entertainment are gaming and the movie business."

Recently, Wal-Mart has quietly circulated word to major-label distribution executives that it will reduce the space devoted to music, perhaps by as much as 20%, in hundreds of its stores. Some record label executives say they have heard similar warnings in the past that have not materialized.

Managers and lawyers who work with record labels say that partly as a result of the big-box squeeze, labels have become more conservative in the kinds of artists they are willing to sign.

For his part, Best Buy's Mr. Arnold says the blame for waning consumer interest in CDs lies with the record labels, not with stores like his. "Music has become a commoditized item," he says. "The CD is perceived by the consumer to be a $10 item, and the manufacturers continue to release new titles at $15 to $18.98." To remedy that situation, he says he has urged labels to move to a "paperback-book model," with no-frills packages priced cheaply for most customers, and more deluxe presentations for die-hard fans.

Chain retailers are unlikely to eliminate music altogether. Big-box chains often set CD prices so low the retailer loses a dollar or two on the most aggressively priced titles. If nothing else, Mr. Arnold readily acknowledges, music remains cheap bait to lure customers who may end up purchasing, say, a brushed-steel refrigerator. "I couldn't imagine Best Buy without music," he says.

EVALUATING THE AUTHOR'S ARGUMENTS:

The author uses many statistics throughout his article. Do you think this is an effective technique? Why or why not?

Big Box Retailers and Record Store Chains Are Not Crushing Indie Stores

"There will always be those that . . . prefer the punk rock ethos of a Newbury Comics to the Deep South values of Wal-Mart."

Michael C. Moynihan

In the following article Michael C. Moynihan argues that, contrary to popular belief, big record chains are not crushing independent record stores. To make his point, he tells the story of a quirky Boston record store called Newbury Comics. Although the store was threatened by incoming retail giants like Tower Records and a Virgin Megastore, Newbury Comics has continued to thrive. Moynihan details several reasons for Newbury's success. For example, although the big stores can offer low prices and a huge selection, the small size of Newbury has made it easier for the owners to react to changes in the market and to cater to their customers' needs. Moynihan is an associate editor of *Reason*, a political journal that covers libertarian issues.

AS YOU READ, CONSIDER THE FOLLOWING QUESTIONS:
1. According to the author, for what reasons did industry experts predict that independent music stores would "feel the pinch" of big box retailers?
2. Name three of the ideas that Moynihan explains Newbury Comics borrowed from the big box model.
3. What two things does the author describe as being "the Achilles' heel" of big box retailers?

On the corner of Newbury Street and Massachusetts Avenue in Boston sits one of the famed architect Frank Gehry's least inspired creations. "360 Newbury" is a big box of a building—appropriate considering that its first three floors have long housed big-box record stores—famous only as Gehry's sole multi-tenant office building in the U.S. But for the third time in 10 years, its retail space sits vacant. Its last tenant, the British-owned music giant Virgin Megastore, broke its lease in 2006 after four unprofitable years hawking CDs and DVDs to local college students. A company spokesman promised "to seek an alternative location in Boston." It has yet to do so.

Virgin snapped up the space in 2002, when the failing music retailer Tower Records vacated the building ahead of its long, protracted descent into bankruptcy. Back in 1987, when Tower Records launched its single largest megastore in the Gehry building, the future of Boston's independent record store business looked grim. Vinyl merchants and industry experts predicted that most independent retailers would feel the pinch of the big box; megastores like Tower would have more stock on hand and, it was presumed, would offer significantly discounted prices. The three-story Tower Records & Video would pose a direct challenge to small, local stores like Newbury Comics, a comic book merchant turned record shop specializing in independent music, hard-to-find imports, and 7-inch records by local bands. To make matters worse, the new Tower store would be situated on the very same block as Newbury Comics.

A Panic over Big Chain Stores

But it wasn't just the specter of Tower that frightened small retailers like Newbury Comics. The music business was experiencing rapid

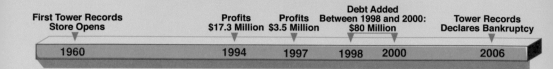

Tower Records Timeline

First Tower Records Store Opens		Profits $17.3 Million	Profits $3.5 Million	Debt Added Between 1998 and 2000: $80 Million		Tower Records Declares Bankruptcy
1960		1994	1997	1998	2000	2006

Taken from: Associated Press, "Tower Records Victim of iPod Era," October 10, 2006. MSNMoney.com. http://articles.moneycentral.msn.com/News/TowerRecordsToClose.aspx?GT1=8618.

growth in compact disc sales, and chain stores were expected to become the dominant players. Giants like Recordtown, Strawberries, Coconuts, Musicland, and Sam Goody—most of whom have now either disappeared or seen influence decline—would come to dominate the industry, *The Boston Globe* predicted. Among independent stores, the *Globe* wrote, a "panic" was precipitating Tower's arrival. So ominous was the thought of a big box music store in Boston that *The New York Times* covered the store's opening, suggesting that the independents might as well throw in the towel, since Tower "has virtually no competition in its league."

At the time, Newbury Comics co-owner Michael Dreese told the *Globe* that he too was "worried," and that when all the chains had settled in—the British giant HMV would soon open a megastore across the river in Cambridge and another in Boston's Downtown Crossing shopping district—"there is going to be blood all over the place." It would, presumably, be the blood of the independents. The *Times* spoke in the past tense, suggesting that the indies' demise was a foregone conclusion. "On the block where a punk-rock record store, Newbury Comics, once held sway," the *Times* sighed, "a new Tower Records sells that kind as well as more mundane music and a wide assortment of videotapes." The store would stock, a spokesman said, "60,000 cassettes and close to 50,000 CDs," versus the typical average of "12,000 CDs and 13,000 cassettes." Who could compete with that?

Well, Newbury Comics, for starters, "We had a huge competitive advantage knowing the local market," Dreese now says. Today Dreese and his partner, both MIT dropouts, preside over a mini-chain of their own, with 27 stores in five states, while HMV, Tower, and Virgin are all distant memories in New England. As the market changed, centrally controlled operations such as the Los Angeles–based Tower proved vulnerable to smaller, more localized competition. "Virgin and Tower were exceptionally poorly managed and made poor use of technology," he says. "Combine that with Virgin and HMV's very British arrogance when they entered the market."

Chains Start to Flounder

As the chains floundered in the face of declining music sales, Newbury Comics nimbly altered its business model without abandoning its core constituency of indie music fans. Today, compact disc sales account for just below 50 percent of Newbury Comics' revenue. DVDs are approximately 20 to 25 percent, and pop culture and sports tschotchkes—Boston Red Sox caps, Ozzy Osbourne action figures—cover the rest. Hiring a platoon of tattooed hipsters added an extra patina of authenticity to the shopping experience—something Virgin, HMV, and Tower didn't offer.

According to Dreese, who spent much of his youth in London hanging around the original Virgin Record Shop's lunch counter, Newbury Comics challenged the big boxes by liberally borrowing from the big-box business model, making aggressive use of "loss leader" merchandise (pricing items below cost to entice customers into the shop), competitive pricing, and a refined distribution system that used vast online data bases. It moved into the Internet early, selling merchandise through both its own website and third-party Web stores such as Amazon and eBay. Dreese doesn't worry much about downloads (iTunes, he says, has helped his business), and, as he recently told *Boston Magazine*, his focus remains on how to "keep beating Wal-Mart."

FAST FACT

The first Record Store Day, in which fans, artists, and record stores celebrated independent record stores, was held in April 2008.

The inability to adapt to local tastes and the failure to anticipate technological market shifts have been the Achilles heel of many big box retailers. When Wal-Mart was forced to shutter its vast network

A customer shops at Newbury Comics in Boston. The store's small size makes it easier for it to react to changes in the marketplace and fulfill its customers' needs.

of German stores, a mystified company spokesman told a reporter: "We thought everyone around the world loved Wal-Mart." (The *International Herald Tribune* quoted a baffled Wal-Mart shopper in South Korea, where the company has also abandoned operations, wondering, "Why would you buy a box of shampoo bottles?") The chain had made the mistake of assuming that full-spectrum retail dominance is achieved by virtue of size alone, without regard to cultural and regional difference.

The Advantage of Being Small

That error is common not just among chains but among their critics. Market leaders do not always react in a timely and profitable manner to shifts in taste and technology. While big-box retailers have enormous competitive advantages—*sui generis* [of its own kind] leverage with distributors and manufacturers, unparalleled capital resources, immense political influence—they also face a distinct disadvantage in adjusting themselves to local preferences. . . .

It is likely true, as big-box critics contend, that stores like Wal-Mart will always dominate certain sectors, thus threatening the existence of many smaller competitors. But chain stores often *create* markets that didn't previously exist, both by forging new trends (like the $10 new release CD, quickly adopted by Newbury Comics) and by provoking a backlash against the alienating experience of big-box shopping. There will always be those that find Wal-Mart inauthentic, those that prefer the punk rock ethos of a Newbury Comics to the Deep South values of Wal-Mart, with its habit of censoring CD covers and song lyrics.

360 Newbury, graveyard of Virgin Megastore and Tower Records, recently announced that it would be renting its first two floors to the electronics and CD retailer Best Buy. After years of doing combat with big boxes, Newbury Comics' Dreese doesn't betray the slightest worry about the latest competitor. "We're the last man standing in Boston," he says. It's a safe bet that, sometime in the near future, he'll be peering down the road, watching another megastore packing a moving van.

EVALUATING THE AUTHOR'S ARGUMENTS:

The author centers his case around the one example of Newbury Comics. Is this an effective tactic? Do you feel that giving one example strengthens or weakens the author's argument? Why?

Chapter 2

How Are New Technologies Affecting Music?

One example of new technologies affecting the music industry is satellite radio. Here, the band 3 Doors Down tapes a show for XM Satellite Radio.

Satellite Radio Will Fail

Rich Duprey

In the following essay Rich Duprey argues that satellite radio is going to fail. Duprey feels that satellite radio's problems can be blamed on three issues: limited play-lists, annoying DJs, and bad reception. He asserts that the vast potential of satellite radio has gone unfulfilled, and that satellite radio executives have made the same mistakes as those of terrestrial radio. Duprey is a frequent contributor to the *Motley Fool*, a publication on investing.

> *"Satellite radio is becoming yesterday's news."*

AS YOU READ, CONSIDER THE FOLLOWING QUESTIONS:
1. What accounts for the bulk of new Sirius radio subscriptions, according to the author?
2. How does Duprey define the term "churn rate"?
3. What are the three ways satellite radio once held a lot of potential, according to Duprey?

S ay goodbye to satellite radio. As a driving force in entertainment, it's already past its heyday. Just as quickly as it exploded on the scene, satellite radio is becoming yesterday's news.

It's not because XM Satellite Radio was able to add only half as many net new subscribers in the first quarter as it did last year. Nor is it because Sirius Satellite Radio added only half a million new subscribers based on the strength of some sketchy new-car production sales schedule (auto manufacturers account for the bulk of new subscribers). Forget that the number of people who buy their satellite radio receivers in-store fell by more than 50% this year and that the churn rates—the number of customers the radio stations lose each month—continue to climb.

No, it's something less statistical than all that, more ephemeral. Satellite radio will fail because it sucks.

I'm not an early adopter of most technology, and I got my first Sirius satellite receiver only when Howard Stern announced that he was leaving terrestrial radio. Being a fan of his comedy, I was willing to test out what a no-holds-barred Stern could be. For the most part, I find his show to be the one bright spot in what has otherwise become a wasteland reminiscent of ground-based stations. Yet one entertainer cannot keep an empire from crumbling.

The biggest problem for satellite radio is that it is morphing into terrestrial radio, albeit without the commercials. Let me list some of the reasons I see satellite radio failing.

- Limited playlists.
- Annoying DJs.
- Lousy reception.

You would think most of those would apply to any terrestrial radio station run by Clear Channel Communications, but they're symptoms of the problem with satellite radio.

Not Enough Variety

I definitely don't miss the insipid commercials I used to find on regular radio, but with 24 hours of airtime to fill up, you'd think the satellite companies could maybe mix up the playlists once in a while. How many times can Sirius' rock station Octane play Hinder's "Lips of an Angel"? And I think there's some Carpenters song played every 12 minutes on its Moving Easy band.

I listen to just a handful of stations on Sirius, and believe me: You can just about set your watch to when a particular song is going to come on. Can't they play some of the lesser-known songs by the

The author thinks that XM Satellite Radio and Sirius Satellite Radio have three things in common: lousy reception, annoying DJs, and limited playlists.

artists, just for variety? While I have a Sirius radio, the same failings apply to XM. Repetitive songs seem to be an industry-wide issue that I thought satellite radio would resolve.

Annoying DJs

Perhaps I'm showing my age, but there's a lot of '70s music I like, so I tune into Totally '70s. I'm left to wonder, though, whether DJ Barry Williams (a.k.a. Greg Brady from *The Brady Bunch*) is required to introduce every song with some pun pulled from a song's lyrics. What terrestrial radio has never learned—and satellite is following closely in its footsteps—is that DJs rarely matter.

Anyone can spin a record. Certain personalities—Howard Stern or Opie & Anthony—are able to differentiate themselves, but then again, they're not playing music. Most DJs are forgettable, even Octane's Kayla, once the music starts.

CBS Radio actually has come to this conclusion. Its nine Jack FM stations—in the New York metro area where I live, it's 101.1—have done away with DJs and simply have a generic, smart-aleck voiceover making commentaries between songs. And the music's not too bad, either, though there are still commercials. Satellite ought to take a cue from CBS.

FAST FACT

Despite the wide variety of music offered on satellite radio, the most popular music stations are hit-based channels like Top 20 and oldies stations.

Poor Reception

I drive the entire length of the New Jersey Turnpike *a lot*. It is exceptionally rare for me to be able to listen to an entire song without the signal cutting out. Sure, you're warned about tall buildings blocking signals sometimes, but there are a lot of flat areas on the turnpike without buildings, trees, or even animals where the receiver suddenly reads "No Signal."

In that respect, I think XM has Sirius beat. You can be deep inside a garage and still get a signal with XM. I've found myself stuck in plenty of dead zones with my Sirius, or I'll be sitting at a traffic light

Actual and Potential Satellite Radio Subscribers

This graph indicates that while the number of actual subscribers to satellite radio has increased, the number of potential subscribers—those asked in a survey how likely they would be to subscribe—has decreased.

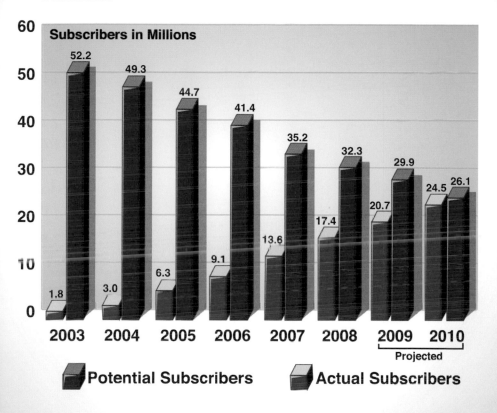

Taken from: Bridge Ratings, February 28, 2007.

inching forward to find just the right spot to get the signal to come back on. Blue skies and green grass might make for great song lyrics, but they're no guarantee of getting a radio signal.

Satellite radio once held a lot of potential: commercial-free, unfettered by the FCC, and able to play whatever the stations wanted. Instead, it's opted for safety. As big-name radio executives like Mel Karmazin moved to satellite, it became more like terrestrial radio.

And when there is little difference between what your local Zoo station is playing—woo-hoo! wheee! yuk! yuk!—and what you can find on satellite, not even a merger of XM and Sirius can save it.

EVALUATING THE AUTHOR'S ARGUMENTS:

Rich Duprey bases most of his argument on his personal impressions of satellite radio. Do you think this technique strengthens or weakens his argument? Why?

Satellite Radio Is a Success

Gael Fashingbauer Cooper

"Satellite radio . . . may not reach cable TV's popularity for years to come, but I believe it's the future."

In the following article Gael Fashingbauer Cooper describes why she thinks satellite radio will be the future of radio. She describes her own experiences with having satellite radio installed in her car. She commends satellite radio's huge variety of station types, especially in music, sports, and talk. She notes that satellite radio, like the Internet, offers programming for practically every conceivable niche audience. Cooper is MSNBC's television and books editor.

AS YOU READ, CONSIDER THE FOLLOWING QUESTIONS:
1. To what does the author equate the twelve dollars per month cost of satellite radio?
2. What advantage does Cooper say satellite radio has in terms of listeners finding out the name of a song and its artist?
3. How many stations of traffic and weather does the author's satellite service provide?

Gael Fashingbauer Cooper, "Why I Love Satellite Radio," MSNBC.com, March 11, 2005. Republished with permission of MSNBC.com, conveyed through Copyright Clearance Center, Inc.

Last week [March 2005] I found myself sitting alone in my parked car in front of my house for about 15 minutes straight. I wasn't talking on the phone, or working on a project. I was listening, rapt, to an episode of science-fiction show "Dimension X," a radio series that aired a dozen years before I was born.

My husband and I added satellite radios to our cars just a few months ago, and like people who finally discover cable TV after years of only having network channels, we're never going back. (What's that the Buggles said, in an oddly prescient song? "We can't rewind, we've gone too far.") Satellite radio may not kill the radio star, and it may not reach cable TV's popularity for years to come, but I believe it's the future.

I support my local independent radio station and am a big fan of public broadcasting, but there are times when there's just nothing on the free dial that I feel like listening to. Not to mention those times when you're in the fifth hour of that long, slow, dull drive up the dusty backbone of California, the basketball game has gone to static, you've memorized all your CDs and the local station plays only scratchy country music from 1974.

Not that satellite radio is cheap. But $12 a month equals one movie ticket, or two magazines, or one month of a pay movie channel like Showtime, or three or four fancy coffees. Considering the amount of time I spend in my car, for me the per-hour enjoyment cost works out. 150 channels is one thing, most of them having absolutely no commercials is an added bonus.

Sinatra to Ska, Jazz to Jam Bands

Whether you end up with XM or Sirius, you can delight in the world of narrowcasting. It's like the Internet: There are Web sites for everyone from "Star Wars" fans to Hummel collectors, because somewhere there's an audience out there for them.

With satellite radio, you can indulge your guilty-pleasure fascination with Broadway songs, or uncensored rap, or gospel music, ska, Euro hits, right-wing or left-wing politics, bluegrass, electronica, Sinatra, opera, classical, jazz, jam bands . . . you name it. On XM alone, there are at least four stations that specialize in one form or another of alternative music. (Soft alternative? Check. Hard alternative? Got it.

A Sampling of the Types of Stations on XM Satellite Radio

Big Band	CNBC
Classic Rock	All Hit Music
Reggae	Hip-Hop
Classic Country	Bloomberg Radio
Acoustic Eclectic Rock	Classic Hits
New and Emerging Music	Contemporary Jazz
Pop Hits of the 1980s	BBC World Service
Grunge/Alternative Rock	Hits of the 2000s
Radio Disney	New Age
Texas Honky Tonk Music	C-SPAN Radio
Jam Bands	Gospel
News and Information	Blues
Bluegrass	NPR News/Conversation
Garage Rock	Heavy Metal
Holiday/Special Occasion	Show Tunes
Folk	Unfiltered Political Talk
Classic Soul	Indie/Underground/Imports
FOX News	Classical
Elvis Presley 24/7	Sports News
Old School R&B	Disco Music
CNN News	Club Music
Top 40	Indy Car Series Racing

Taken from: XM Radio, March 2009.

90s and Today's Alternative? Sure. Deep Classic Alternative? Not sure what that is, but they've got that too.)

Both major satellite services also allow listeners to take a tour through the ages via decade-specific music stations. Flip from the wartime hits of the 1940s to 1950s rockabilly to 1960s Brit rock to 1970s soft tunes to 1980s pop to 1990s . . . whatever 1990s music means to you. I most often switch between the ballady 1940s channel (the music my GI parents imbued me with) to the 1980s hits of my high-school days ("I was on the Paris train, I emerged in London rain"). Unsure exactly what song that is? Satellite radio flashes the name of the song and artist across the screen, so I no longer have to try and remember a scrap of lyric until I can hunt down the singer's name online.

Keeping in Touch with Home

The satellite service I subscribe to also provides 20+ stations of 24-7 traffic and weather news for major U.S. cities. While I live and drive in Seattle, I have one of my preset radio buttons set to the station for my hometowns of Minneapolis-St. Paul. When I'm homesick, I still get a kick out of hearing the old freeway names and interchanges I once knew so well. And on a gray Seattle winter day, temperatures in the 40s seem a lot warmer when I push the button for MSP and see "TEMPERATURE: SEVENTEEN BELOW" flashing across the screen.

FAST FACT

The highest-rated satellite radio channel is Howard Stern 100 on Sirius Radio.

Satellite radio also offers endless talk stations. Personally, I'll never listen to Howard Stern or any of the other extreme jocks. But I still find it entertaining that, in addition to right-wing and left-wing political chatter, there's a Christian talk station, an African-American talk station, and a trucker's channel.

There are numerous comedy stations, including one that keeps it G-rated for when the family's in the car, and my favorite, the old-time radio show station. It can be tough to get out of the car at the grocery store when an episode of "Dragnet" is on, but fortunately, my radio unit allows me to pause and replay up to 30 minutes of programming. (Think TiVo for radio!)

Sports fans who subscribe to a satellite TV service such as Direct TV already know they can get football or baseball games from around the league. Satellite radio offers the same thing, depending on the service you choose, with different sports available on different services.

I'm not the biggest sports fan, but if my hometown Twins ever get those Homer Hankies [a special handkerchief waved by fans of the Minnesota Twins] waving again, I can cruise around and tune in to their every game as if they weren't 1500 miles away.

The Sound Quality Is Fine

I've heard people complain about the quality of satellite radio, but that's usually about the point in the discussion where I completely tune out. It sounds fine to me, but then I'm not the kind of person who spends hours geeking out in expensive audio-video stores drooling over the expensive equipment. (I've been known to listen to—gasp—AM radio with nary or little problem.) Can I hear it? Yes. Can I understand it? Yes. Does it drop out? Not even in tunnels and underground parking garages. So I'll leave the technical debates to the geeks.

The author argues that satellite radio's big advantage is a large number of channels that broadcast specific genres of music, sports, and talk.

In the 10 years I've been married, my husband and I have driven cross-country twice, around the Deep South once, and had numerous long car trips between Seattle and Los Angeles. I love those drives and I love the company, but really, an hour outside of Bakersfield the boredom rolls in like an endlessly turning tumbleweed.

Closer to home, when an accident or random traffic jam stops up my commute, the car seems less like a Honda Civic and more like a prison. But now I can tune into "Dragnet," or an old Steve Martin comedy routine, or the BBC, or the unsigned bands station. The miles still have to be crossed, but they go by a little easier.

EVALUATING THE AUTHOR'S ARGUMENTS:

In the article, the author uses an informal tone and does not cite any statistics or experts. Do you think that this weakens her argument or makes it more accessible? Explain your answer.

Artists Should Decide Whether iTunes Offers Singles or Albums

"We get so caught up in technology and ease [of downloading a single] . . . there's nothing wrong with listening to a whole record from start to finish."

Ray Waddell

Kid Rock has always been a rebel. Even when iTunes became one of the most popular ways of obtaining a quick tune for the everyday consumer, according to the following viewpoint, Kid Rock even rebels against that. The artist contends that his fans will obtain what they want no matter how convenient iTunes is. Kid Rock also tells the author that he would only sell what is relevant to him and his lifestyle. Ray Waddell is a contributing writing for Billboard.com.

AS YOU READ, CONSIDER THE FOLLOWING QUESTIONS:
1. According to the author, what else is Kid Rock a critic of?
2. According to the president of Atlantic, at which sites could a fan purchase Kid Rock's album?
3. Why does Kid Rock say "you probably won't see me on a Wheaties box or selling Tide detergent . . ."? What is different about these products than the ones Kid Rock chooses to endorse?

Kid Rock's latest album "Rock'n'Roll Jesus" and its single "All Summer Long" have been two of the biggest hits of the summer. But it's happened without either being available for download via Apple's iTunes Music Store in the United States.

Playing His Own Tune

Rock has been an outspoken critic not only of track downloading but Internet piracy. In a "smartass" public service announcement he

Musicians like Kid Rock are fighting to maintain control over the use of their music on iTunes.

Artists Who Have Boycotted iTunes

- Jay-Z
- Kid Rock
- The Beatles
- Radiohead
- AC/DC
- Garth Brooks

Taken from: Ian Youngs, "Kid Rock Boycotts iTunes Over Pay," BBC, June 18, 2008.

recently advised people to steal everything. Eschewing iTunes also proves a point, Rock adds.

"I tell people in my organization, 'Do not ever come up to me and say, "This is what everyone's doing and how they're doing it." Don't ever give me that lame-ass bullsh*t,'" he tells *Billboard* at a Nashville tequila bar. "As soon as someone says, 'You have to be on iTunes . . . they're the No. 1 retailer' . . . I don't have to. Because I remember being a kid when I heard a song that I liked, I would jump on the bus, ride to Detroit, get a $2.50 transfer and walk a mile to the hip-hop store to buy the new Eric B. & Rakim record. You're not going to stop people from obtaining what they want if it's available at some level."

FAST FACT

Sales of entire albums, including digital albums, dropped 15 percent in 2007, while single-track sales rose 45 percent.

However, Atlantic president Julie Greenwald says "Rock'n'Roll Jesus" will be available soon digitally in the States as an album via providers like Amazon, walmart.com, Rhapsody and bestbuy.com.

"We get so caught up in technology and ease [of downloading a single] . . . there's nothing wrong with listening to a whole record from start to finish," Kid Rock co-manager Ken Levitan says.

Kid Rock Promotes His Interests

In other news, Kid Rock and his Twisted Brown Trucker band recently cut a new song, "Warrior," for a National Guard commercial. It will be downloadable in its entirety on the National Guard's Web site once the commercial airs. He's also looking at launching signature beer and cigar products.

"I like [branding opportunities] when it's something I'm into, and I'm definitely into beer and cigars," Rock says. "You probably won't see me on the cover of a Wheaties box or selling Tide detergent, because it's irrelevant to me."

EVALUATING THE AUTHOR'S ARGUMENTS:

Consider the Web sites the author mentioned Atlantic would sell Kid Rock's new album on. Compare these sites to iTunes Music Store. What are the differences? Why do you think Kid Rock would be willing to sell on these sites but not iTunes?

Viewpoint 4

Consumers Should Decide Whether iTunes Offers Singles or Albums

"We're not opposed to the concept of giving artists choice, but consumer choice is important, too."

Charles Starrett

The following selection was written in response to an article by Jermaine Dupri arguing that iTunes should sell entire albums, not singles. Starrett takes the opposite stance, asserting that both albums and singles should be available. According to Starrett, consumers should be free to buy as much or as little of an artist's work as they would like. He suggests that the movement to limit iTunes to album sales is not actually about helping artists, but instead just another way for record companies to make money. After all, if record companies can charge consumers for a whole album when the buyer just wants one song, the record company will make a much higher profit. Starrett is a senior editor at *iLounge*, a Web magazine dedicated to coverage of iPods and iPhones.

AS YOU READ, CONSIDER THE FOLLOWING QUESTIONS:
 1. What are the three types of stores Starrett lists where consumers buy music?
 2. According to the author, what incentive does iTunes offer to encourage full album sales?
 3. How many songs purchased from the iTunes Store does the average iPod contain, according to the author?

In today's music industry, few names are as important as those of Jermaine Dupri, the well-known rapper, producer and president of Island Urban Records, and Shawn Carter, also known as Jay-Z, the hugely successful recording artist who also serves as the president of Def Jam Recordings and Roc-A-Fella Records. Success aside, both men have something in common: they both work for Universal Music Group, whose president, Doug Morris, has been waging a public, nasty campaign against Apple's iTunes Store.

Until recently, Dupri and Jay-Z have been quietly enjoying all the cash that iTunes has been funneling to their labels, but this month, both artists became soldiers in Morris's battle against iTunes, publicly attacking the Store's policy of offering 99-cent singles in addition to whole album purchases. Carter began by unexpectedly yanking his new movie-inspired album *American Gangster* from iTunes well after pre-orders had been piling up, stating that, "As movies are not sold scene by scene, this collection will not be sold as individual singles." Then Dupri followed Carter's lead, writing in a blog post that Apple should allow artists to choose whether to sell whole albums or singles and albums.

We're not opposed to the concept of giving artists choice, but consumer choice is important, too, and that's an important point that Universal's executives still just don't seem to understand. There are lots of stores selling music these days: online and bricks-and-mortar stores with CDs and DVDs, and online stores with digital downloads. Some offer only a handful of full albums. Some stock singles. And some, like Apple's iTunes Store, sell both full albums and singles. Consumers buy from all three types of stores, and vote with their pocketbooks as to what they prefer. Should an artist or recording

Top Ten Albums and Songs Downloaded at iTunes

The best-selling albums of 2007, according to Apple:

1. Maroon 5 - *It Won't Be Soon Before Long*
2. Amy Winehouse - *Back to Black*
3. Kanye West - *Graduation*
4. Daughtry - *Daughtry*
5. Colbie Caillat - *Coco*
6. Linkin Park - *Minutes to Midnight*
7. Various Artists - High School Musical 2 *Soundtrack*
8. Timbaland - *Timbaland Presents: Shock Value*
9. John Mayer - *Continuum*
10. Various Artists - Hairspray *Soundtrack*

The best-selling songs of 2007, according to Apple:

1. Fergie - "Big Girls Don't Cry (Personal)"
2. Gwen Stefani - "The Sweet Escape"
3. Plain White T's - "Hey There Delilah"
4. Avril Lavigne - "Girlfriend"
5. Fergie - "Glamorous"
6. Kanye West - "Stronger"
7. Maroon 5 - "Makes Me Wonder"
8. Akon - "Don't Matter"
9. Timbaland (featuring Keri Hilson & D.O.E.) - "The Way I Are"
10. Shop Boyz - "Party Like a Rock Star"

Taken from: James Montgomery, "Fergie, Maroon 5, Amy Winehouse Are iTune's Most Downloaded Artists of 2007,"
MTV.com, December 11, 2007.

executive really be attacking a store if the way it does business has proved to be increasingly popular?

What inspired this editorial was a set of comments from Dupri, who didn't just attack the iTunes Store, but went further, attacking consumers, too—clear evidence that there are still out-of-touch record executives left in this increasingly digital age. There are plenty of choice quotes that we could highlight, but none was more offensive than this description of how to manipulate consumers to spur album sales:

> We let the consumer have too much of what they want, too soon, and we hurt ourselves. Back in the day when people were excited about a record coming out we'd put out a single to get the ball going and if we sold a lot of singles that was an indication we'd sell a lot of albums. But we'd cut the single off a few weeks before the album came out to get people to wait and let the excitement build. When I put out Kris Kross we did that. We sold two million singles, then we stopped. Eventually we sold eight million albums! Did consumers complain? Maybe so. But at what point does any business care when a consumer complains about the money?

Customers Are a Record Company's "Lifeblood"

Thankfully, there's a simple answer for Mr. Dupri: the point at which a business should care about consumers is "always." They are your lifeblood. They are the only reason you make money. And you should be especially sensitive to their complaints at the point at which your business is losing traction, declining in revenues, and succumbing to piracy. Thanks to artists like Mr. Dupri's Kris Kross, which released albums with two popular songs and a bunch of tracks no one cared about before disappearing from the industry, that's exactly where Universal Music Group was before iTunes, and where it will be again if it continues the practices that led to iTunes' astounding popularity.

Dupri's rant, like Jay-Z's decision to pull *American Gangster* from iTunes, is premised on the inaccurate suggestion that record companies can still force someone to pay $10–15 for a collection of content that only holds $1–3 of value to them. Even more foolishly, it states specifically that companies can offer a $1 song for a brief period of time, then yank it to encourage people to spend $10–15 to buy the same song again with the rest of an album.

This goes without saying, but in today's world, if a company tries to "cut the single off," all it will accomplish is boosting illegal downloads of the track. Consumers today demand instant access to the media they want, so if companies decide not to let them have it legally, they will find another way to get it. Or they simply won't listen at all. iTunes, like the sale of singles on albums, cassettes, or CDs, enables consumers to pay artists a fair amount for the tracks they like, rather than paying nothing for an album where the chaff grossly outweighs the wheat. And unlike any old fashioned record store, it incentivizes full album sales by offering credits for previously downloaded tracks from an album, rather than forcing consumers to buy the same song twice.

Though Dupri and Jay-Z have suggested that full album sales are important to an artist's mission of delivering a complete body of work at the same time, it's obvious that this really is about squeezing more money out of consumers, using guilt or any other rationalization that's convenient. Another choice quote from Dupri is this one:

"Why do people not care how we—the people who make music—eat?"

Let's be fair here. We've seen *MTV Cribs*—we know what your house looks like. Please don't tell us that you need to sell full albums in order to "eat"; if so, you've either been an incredibly unlucky investor, or you burn more cash in a week than most people could in 10 lifetimes. You're one of the ten richest people in hip-hop, with an estimated net worth of $60 million. So let's leave you out of any discussion concerning artists that actually rely on album sales to survive—of course, that's if you actually believe that the artists see any large portion of the money from album sales, which they don't.

Also enjoyable was Dupri's description of Apple's downfall, should the labels decide to pull their music from the iTunes Store:

> If anything, WE made iTunes. It's like how we spent $300,000 to $500,000 each on our videos and MTV and BET went ahead and built an entire video television industry off of our backs. We can't let that happen again. These businesses exist solely because of our music. So if we as artists, producers and label executives stand up, those guys at Apple can either cooperate, or have nothing for people to buy and download on their iPods.

> Apple thinks that's never gonna happen. They think that we as the record industry will never stick together. But Universal sells one out of every three records. All it'll take is for Warner Music to say, "You know what, I'm with you," for us to shut 'em down. No more iPods! They won't have nothin' to play on their players!

Shutting Down iTunes Will Not Help Artists

The statement is both generally and specifically absolutely laughable. Statistics show that the average iPod contains only a handful of songs purchased from the iTunes Store, which makes it pretty clear that the success of the iPod doesn't depend on the Store—it's a component of the iPod ecosystem, yes, but hardly the focus. Again, the only thing shutting down the iTunes Store is going to achieve is driving more consumers to the world of BitTorrent and illegal downloads. Of course, iPods play more than what's available on the Store. And yes, MTV and BET built networks on the backs of musicians, but so did radio, and satellite radio after that, and without the ability to flood those entertainment channels with your music, you'd be selling *way* fewer records. How would you have gotten your $300,000 to $500,000 videos out to your potential fans without MTV, BET, iTunes and others? Don't blame Apple—they were hardly the first to profit from connecting fans with artists, and they will most certainly not be the last.

iLounge's editors have a lot of respect for Jermaine Dupri and Jay-Z as recording artists. Dupri's history of famous tracks speaks for itself, and his Chingy collaboration song "Right Thurr" was featured

The author argues that consumers, not the record labels or musicians, should decide whether or not to download singles or whole albums by the artists.

on iLounge's Backstage page as one of our editors' favorite songs. Jay-Z's albums, including *American Gangster*, have repeatedly been mentioned on Backstage, featured in our photographs, and enjoyed by our editors as well. But as executives, these guys are on the wrong side of history. Trying to use guilt and other tricks to make more money off of music is a losing strategy, and ignorant of the reality that consumers have other options, both with respect to listening to their music, and ignoring it in favor of other artists and labels.

The days of music industry gimmicks are over. In our view, artists should be glad when people think their work is worth paying for—as an anthology, or in pieces—and the moguls that promote them should be open-minded to the reality that the business has changed from buffet to a la carte pricing. If JD and Jay-Z really have a problem with selling singles, fine, don't sell them. It's perfectly fair for an artist to decide how his/her work is distributed, but don't blame the consumer for making it clear that this is not the way he or she wants to enjoy your work, or iTunes for catering to those consumers rather than ignoring them.

EVALUATING THE AUTHOR'S ARGUMENTS:

The author writes for a Web site devoted to covering iPods and iPhones. Although the Web site is not affiliated with Apple Computer, does the site's focus on Apple products make you more or less apt to accept the author's argument? Do you think this gives him an undue bias one way or the other? Why or why not?

Viewpoint

5

Radiohead's Pay-What-You-Want Experiment Is Bad for Business

Andrew Moylan

"If the Radiohead model proves successful, it could mark a turning point for the big record companies."

According to the following viewpoint, since the arrival of online file-sharing programs like Napster, then the appearance of the iTunes Music Store, the downturn of record companies has been inevitable. Andrew Moylan discusses the ways today's artists avoid using record companies in order to sell cheaper music to their fans. Moylan cites record company executives who believe that business is waning. Moylan is government affairs manager at the National Taxpayers Union.

AS YOU READ, CONSIDER THE FOLLOWING QUESTIONS:

1. According to Moylan, what did Madonna do in order to turn a profit? Within this viewpoint, why is making a profit through alternate means bad for record companies and their business?

2. What happened when Radiohead cut the record companies out of their selling and distributing process altogether?
3. According to Moylan, when an artist uses conventional selling methods through a major label, how much does the artist/band make per album? How does Radiohead turn a higher profit from its pay-what-you-want model?

The British mega-band Radiohead made headlines last month by releasing its new album "In Rainbows" exclusively for download on its website and allowing consumers to set their own prices. Such an unusual and direct challenge to the music industry instantly made headlines—but it may be a portent of things to come.

Downturn for Record Companies Is Now a Reality

Nine Inch Nails has pledged to follow Radiohead's example when its current record deal ends. Prince included 2.5 million copies of his new album in a popular British Sunday newspaper, and handed it out for free to attendees of his concert, much to the consternation of record executives. Madonna made news recently by signing with a concert promotion firm in order to focus on live performances, endorsements, and merchandising, rather than on traditional album sales. More and more, recorded music is becoming a mere promotional tool for other profitable musical endeavors, such as live concerts. If this trends gains momentum, it could spell the end of the music industry as we know it.

FAST FACT

Fortune magazine ranked Radiohead's pay-what-you-want experiment with *In Rainbows* number 59 in their 2007 list of the 101 Dumbest Moments in Business.

Radiohead has created the potential for a whole new system of music distribution in which consumers set the prices.

Much has been written about the impending demise of the large record labels, some of it exaggerated. But the numbers don't lie: in the first half of 2007, CD sales were down by 19.3 percent when compared to the same period in 2006. As author Frederic Dannen has pointed out, music consumers have consistently chosen convenience as the most important factor in selecting a medium, and the industry has been extremely slow to catch on. No longer are consumers forced to purchase entire albums to hear the one song they like, nor must they purchase an expensive "CD single." Innovations such as downloading of albums and cheap single-song purchases continue to chip away at industry profits. It started with Napster and other file-sharing programs (some of which were legal but most of which were not), progressed with the iTunes music store and Internet-based retailers, and has culminated with Radiohead's online-only album release.

The band Radiohead's decision to make their recent album available for download via the Internet for whatever price the consumer wants to pay is bad for the business because it devalues the music, according to the author.

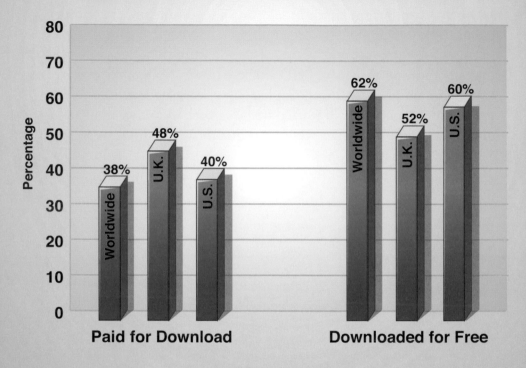

Radiohead *In Rainbows* Online Album Downloads, October 1–29, 2007

Paid for Download
- Worldwide 38%
- U.K. 48%
- U.S. 40%

Downloaded for Free
- Worldwide 62%
- U.K. 52%
- U.S. 60%

Percentage

Taken from: comScore, November 8, 2007.

The Radiohead Model

If the Radiohead model proves successful, it could mark a turning point for the big record companies. Though much-reviled, they do provide valuable services for many bands. They use their connections and expertise to advertise, secure distribution, and aggressively promote music heard on the radio and elsewhere. But now that Radiohead is firmly established, it has little need for these services. By cutting the record companies out of the process altogether, the band has reduced its initial production cost—which means cheaper music for the fans.

Radiohead has thus created the potential for a whole new system of music distribution—one that is controlled through a band's own website—in which consumers set the prices. Indeed, Radiohead fans can pay whatever price they want to purchase a digital download of

"In Rainbows." Some may pay nothing for the record, but many will pay a price they feel is fair because they know their money is going directly to the band. Meanwhile, Radiohead is spared the typical advertising and distribution costs.

What Goes to the Band, What's Left for Labels

The *Wall Street Journal* has estimated that the average cost to deliver an album's worth of music online could be as low as $3.40, compared with an average cost of roughly $6.40 to deliver it in traditional CD format. When using conventional methods, major label bands make roughly $1.00 per album sold. So even if the average payment for Radiohead's new album is less than $5.00, the band could still turn a higher profit from its online-only release than it would have through traditional album distribution.

Record industry bigwigs have reacted to this turn of events with a mixture of skepticism and horror. Some have expressed doubt about its potential, pointing out that profits from successful albums are used to subsidize up-and-coming artists. But one executive at a big European music label told *Time* magazine that it felt like "yet another death knell" for the industry. "If the best band in the world doesn't want a part of us," the executive added, "I'm not sure what's left for this business."

What will be "left for this business" is the same set of choices facing anyone in a free-market system: adapt, innovate, or lose market share. Time will tell which of these actions the record industry takes.

EVALUATING THE AUTHOR'S ARGUMENTS:

The author focuses on alternative ways artists turn a profit. Why do you think he does this? How do these points support the argument?

Viewpoint 6

Radiohead's Pay-What-You-Want Experiment Is Just a New Way of Doing Business

"Radiohead hasn't created a radical new model. They've merely served up an additional option."

Fred Mills

In the following article Fred Mills examines the excitement among the media, fans, and musicians surrounding the release of Radiohead's pay-what-you-want experiment of their album *In Rainbows*. In Mills's view, the event was overanalyzed and overhyped, and it caused excessive worry in the music world. The release of *In Rainbows* does not change the face of the music industry, Mills argues. Instead, the downloading experiment just provides bands with another method of promoting their music. Mills is the books editor for *Harp*.

AS YOU READ, CONSIDER THE FOLLOWING QUESTIONS:

1. How many downloads were there in the first two days after the release of *In Rainbows,* according to media estimates?
2. According to the author, what did Radiohead guitarist Jonny Greenwood say was the reason the band released the album in the pay-what-you-want format?
3. What are some of the options the author suggests for bands to reach their fan base and promote themselves?

Whew. That pounding in your temples? It's not the tequila-and-schnapps chasers you were pounding back last night at the transvestite bar—that's the sound of 1.2 million bloggers, media analysts, music industry talking heads and java hut armchair pundits yammering on and on and on about Radiohead. And it doesn't look like the hangover's going away anytime soon.

You know—Radiohead. That obscure indie band from Great Britain who shocked the world a couple of weeks ago [October 2007] when they announced that, newly free of indenture to a mega-corporation (that's record label to you, pal), they would be relcasing their new album *In Rainbows* digitally on Oct. 10 [2007] and that consumers could essentially pick the price they were willing to pay for the digital version. (You could additionally pre-order a hard-copy edition, due in November, that would contain vinyl and expanded CD versions of the album, with the price coming out to about $80 in American currency.)

For the record, I paid £ 2.00, which with the £ 0.45 credit card transaction fee, came to a total of £ 2.45—about $4.97. Full disclosure: to me that seems about five dollars too high for a musical artifact that comes with no packaging whatsoever and, with MP3s at a mere 160kbps, offers sound quality substantially inferior to anything in my vinyl, CD or 8-track tape collection. Factor in 10 cents for some card stock paper (to print out some bootleg artwork I found on the web for the album, natch) and another 30 cents or so for a CDR to burn *In Rainbows* to, and I've forked about close to five and a half bucks. I didn't even get the proverbial "lousy tee-shirt" to show off my bragging rights.

How Much Did Staff Members at *New York* Magazine Pay for *In Rainbows*?

Number of Staffers

6
5
4
3
2
1
0

$0 $5 $8 $10 $14 $20

Price Paid

Taken from: *New York* magazine, October 10, 2007.

Some Pay Nothing, Some Pay Top Price

Out there in the real world, a survey by England's Telegraph.co.uk of 5,000 fans who downloaded the album revealed that "more than a quarter—1,429—paid either nothing or 1p [pence] for the recordings. More than half—2,776—gave up to £10, while 673 die-hard fans paid £ 40 for the deluxe box set." And a few nuts paid £ 99.99, which was the maximum price you could pay. I'm not sure what category my £ 2.45 lands me in—borderline skinflint but still relatively sane, maybe?

Griping aside, though, the whole experience of obtaining the album was painless and seamless; I put in my quarter, pulled the lever, and ten digital gumballs spiraled down and popped out the chute onto my desktop in less than a minute. (Record labels who service journalists with digital promos and make us wade through all manner of cumbersome, time-consuming procedures just to obtain lousy-sounding approximations of their artists' latest magnum opi [a made-up plural of *magnum opus,* meaning a great work of art] should take heed.)

Plus, it's a pretty damn good record, one that brings elements of classic-period Radiohead (e.g., *OK Computer*) to the table alongside touches of Thom Yorke's solo album *The Eraser* and a raft of surprises as well. To paraphrase one reviewer, Radiohead's become Britain's premier art-rock band, and on this occasion the "art" contingent in the Radiohead camp definitely held sway over the band's rockers. The album will undoubtedly figure prominently on a lot of year-end Top Ten lists. . . .

A "Fantastic Experiment for Radiohead"

So anyway . . . media types who track this sort of stuff are estimating that Radiohead moved about 1.2 million downloads across two days. An insider "close to the band" is being cited as the source for that figure, said insider also suggesting that the financial tally was £4.8 million in sales (not counting the pre-orders for the discbox set). Not a bad payday. Chris Hufford, one of the band's managers, told British reporters, "This has been an absolutely fantastic experiment for Radiohead. I can't say what fans have been paying for the new album but it's definitely the case that more people have paid for it than not."

FAST FACT

A Web site called Aralie.com has adopted Radiohead's pay-what-you-want idea and offers music from independent bands as a low-risk way to discover new music.

It's worth noting, however, that worldwide navel gazing and brow furrowing notwithstanding, Radiohead guitarist Jonny Greenwood essentially stated the other day that it was never Radiohead's intention to initiate some revolutionary new model of music distribution (labels have been selling downloads for some time, duh) or even to give away its music as part of some elaborate marketing scheme, but simply to prevent it from leaking out to the public prior to the official

Radiohead guitarist Jonny Greenwood has said that it was not the band's intent to revolutionize music distribution but to prevent their music from leaking out for free prior to its release.

release of the physical discbox. Radiohead is also apparently hoping that fans who dig what they hear on the MP3 files will be convinced to purchase the real thing in all its elaborate packaging and up-to-snuff sonics. I think Greenwood's comments are astute; Radiohead *is* the type of band who commands a fierce loyalty among fans, the type of fans who probably will want to own the physical product. Me, a Luddite [an opponent of technological progress] who has zero-to-none interest in downloading and listening to crappy-sounding compressed music, will want to own at least the official standalone CD when it comes out in early 2008 on an as-yet-unspecified label that some industry watchers are predicting will be Side One Recordings/ATO.

Different Models for Different Bands

There's already been some backlash (not to mention a lot of meta-navel gazing in response to the backlash . . . double whew . . . sometimes a 160kbps MP3 is just a 160kbps MP3, Dr. Freud!) as people trot out, once again, the "what is music worth to consumers?" rhetoric. Over in the Portishead camp—the UK band reportedly has a new album just about completed—we heard complaints that while it's fine and dandy for an established superstar like Radiohead or Prince to give its music away for free, what about lower-tiered acts who can't necessarily make the same gamble that Greenwood suggests? But that argument is moot; if you believe the industry narrative of the past few years, peer-to-peer file sharing has already "devalued" music.

So Radiohead hasn't created a radical new model. They've merely served up an additional option. If we've learned anything lately, it's that there's no one-size-fits-all "model" for bands. There are myriad avenues with which they can travel to reach their fanbase and earn a living, from the tried and true Get In The Van method, to working that MySpace presence like a motherf---er, to flogging music via ads and TV/film placement, to virtual performances in Second Life, and of course to the Radiohead Method.

You know, in the end, dwelling endlessly on all this—the "narrative" and all its tendrils—is a big distraction that takes away from that quaint little notion known as "quality listening time." To quote the great philosophers at Stiff Records: f--- art, let's dance.

EVALUATING THE AUTHOR'S ARGUMENTS:

The author uses a very informal tone, including swearing, casual phrasing, and jokes. Does this affect the author's authority and thus the power of his argument? Are you more likely to be persuaded by this style or by a more formal approach? Why?

Chapter 3

What Should the Rules Be for Downloading Music and Paying Artists?

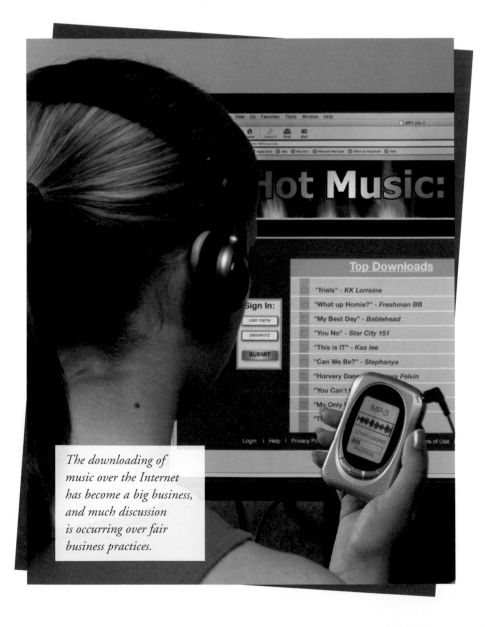

The downloading of music over the Internet has become a big business, and much discussion is occurring over fair business practices.

Illegally Downloading Music Is Wrong

Editorial Board, Music Industry Piracy Investigations

"Asserting that music should be free is the same as saying it has no value."

The following viewpoint was written by the Editorial Board of Music Industry Piracy Investigations (MIPI), an Australian organization that conducts investigative, preventative, and educational activities in relation to music piracy. MIPI equates illegal downloading with stealing, and points out that illegal downloads hurt more than just rich rock stars or faceless corporations. Countless workers, including album art designers and various sound technicians, depend on the profits from musicians' creative works. The author also notes the high expenses musicians incur and points out that musicians, like bus drivers or office workers, are professionals and deserve to be paid.

AS YOU READ, CONSIDER THE FOLLOWING QUESTIONS:
1. The author asserts that artists take a financial risk in making music. What are the financial expenses the author mentions?
2. The author explains that many workers in the music industry are negatively affected by illegal downloading. Name three of the jobs affected.
3. What are three ways, according to the article, in which people can respect copyright?

Do you wonder why on earth you should care about ripping music off the internet or illegally burning CDs or DVDs? Well, perhaps you should consider some of the reasons set out below.

A lot of people who copy and distribute music illegally try to rationalize their behavior by arguing that the people who make music are all rich anyway, and that music should be free for everyone. But asserting that music should be free is the same as saying it has no value—that music is worthless. It's not.

Music doesn't just happen. It's written, bar by bar, line by line, by people who work hard to get it right.

Artists Work Hard

For the artist, the hard work requires not only a major emotional and intellectual commitment, but also long hours, intense concentration, and real financial risk. There's a lot of imagination, soul, and courage involved in creative work. But making music is also a career for artists and getting an income is as important as it is for anyone working in an office, driving a bus or running a company. It's about putting food on the table and covering the rent. It's about making enough money to pay for all that equipment and rehearsal time, about keeping yourself afloat as you strive to succeed in a highly competitive industry.

What gives the music value is not only that you like it, but also that you buy it. If you steal it, you're not just stealing from a record company. You're stealing from the very artists you respect and admire who put all that hard work and energy into giving you their music.

> People should realise that having the recordings of music that other people have made is a privilege and not a right. People use the excuse that it's okay to steal music because making music isn't real work because artists have fun doing it. Well, there's good gigs and bad gigs just like there's good and bad days at work. If you apply that principle, when I have a run of packing some particularly good boxes (alas, that's what I do for money to support myself) and feel particularly satisfied one day then I should be paid less for that time! Absurd! Intrinsic rewards don't pay the bills. —KIM SALMON

New Artists Need a Gig

Music piracy hurts established artists and does even more damage to up-and-coming artists because it deprives the Australian music industry of the revenue needed to finance the huge costs of finding and developing new Australian talent.

People often say that illegal copying is a victimless crime that really doesn't hurt anyone. Try telling that to the struggling young musicians in a garage band who can't get signed because record sales are down. Or tell it to the young singer-songwriter whose career dead-ends because people would rather download her music for free.

There's no question that internet exposure can be a great thing for new artists. For many up-and-coming bands, there's no better way of getting noticed and establishing a following than creating a

A teenager downloads music off the Internet onto his iPod. The author argues that illegally downloading music is morally wrong.

website and putting your stuff out there for the online world to hear. But there's a difference between checking out a band that chooses to let people download its music for free and deciding for yourself that somebody's music should be spread all over the internet.

Making records is an expensive undertaking. So is building a career. If people aren't willing to pay for the music they love, record companies both big and small will find it increasingly difficult to commit the kind of resources it takes to discover and develop new talent.

> Even buskers [street performers] get paid for playing music. Sitting on their arse on the street. But it's better to have a choice as to how you experience music. You can hear music on your radio or on your iPod or see and hear an artist in a club. It takes some money to get off the footpath and to get to all those other places. Nothing is free. Everything is plugged in. The money gets around and for the artists, nothing gets wasted, believe me.
> —DAVE GRANEY

Illegal Downloading Is Unfair

It's unfair to the entire artistic community that creates music. It's unfair to the singer/songwriters who get their copyrights plundered. It's unfair to the musicians who are deprived of their dream of making a living from their art. It's unfair for the owners of small record stores which will close because of the substantial revenue losses.

FAST FACT

Ruckus, a multimedia network service, offers over 3 million free and legal downloads to college students at affiliated schools.

Songwriters and artists, whether established or up-and-coming, aren't the only people hurt by illegal copying. In Australia alone there are thousands of people employed in the music industry—and very few of them are rich rock stars. Stealing music also threatens the livelihoods of the thousands of technicians, CD-plant workers, warehousemen, graphic designers, printers and other non-musicians who are employed in the music business helping to create and deliver the music you listen to.

Willingness to Commit Illegal Acts

This graph shows survey responses to the following question: If you knew that you could get away with it without getting caught or facing any consequences whatsoever, which of the following would you be willing to do?

Percent Willing

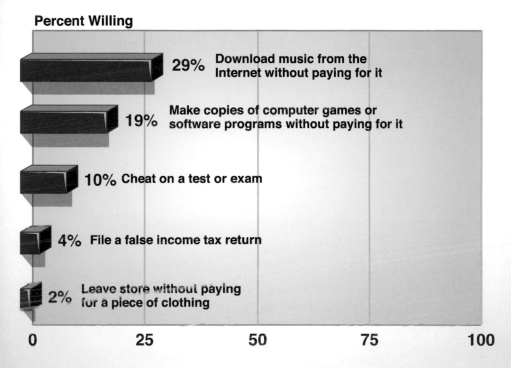

29% Download music from the Internet without paying for it

19% Make copies of computer games or software programs without paying for it

10% Cheat on a test or exam

4% File a false income tax return

2% Leave store without paying for a piece of clothing

| 0 | 25 | 50 | 75 | 100 |

Taken from: ENVIRONICS, September 2006.

Isn't it more exciting to own the real artwork and CD and hold it in your hands? —KAV TEMPERLEY, ESKIMO JOE

Illegal Downloading Is Wrong

You wouldn't steal a mobile phone or t-shirt. Our sense of right and wrong keeps most of us from doing such a thing. Sure, we know there are criminal penalties, but the main reason we don't steal is because we know it's wrong.

Yet when it comes to stealing music, people somehow seem to think the same rules don't apply. Well they do.

Downloading can be a great way to share music, but downloading music illegally threatens the future of everyone that depends on you for their livelihood. Get music the right way! If you download, do it legally! —KEITH URBAN

We want to encourage you to do the right thing—to let you know what's okay and what isn't; to educate fans about who really gets hurt when they steal music; and to show computer users who want to download music from the Internet how to do it legally.

Our message is simple. **Stealing music is the same as stealing anything else.** It is illegal and the consequences are real, for artists, songwriters, you, and for the future of music.

So enjoy the music artists bring you, but please respect copyright. Stop burning multiple copies for friends! Stop offering to upload music files to millions of users on the Internet! Stop downloading from unauthorized sites!

EVALUATING THE AUTHOR'S ARGUMENTS:

This viewpoint does not rely on statistics, and instead makes an appeal to human decency. In your opinion, is this an effective tactic? Why or why not?

Illegally Downloading Music Is a Necessary Evil

Andy Cochrane

> "We steal because it is easier, not because it is cheaper, so make it easier to buy your products."

In the following selection Andy Cochrane addresses the Motion Picture Association of America (MPAA) and the Recording Industry Association of America (RIAA), which are the overseeing organizations for the movie and music businesses. Cochrane understands these industries' frustration with people illegally downloading, and he makes several suggestions as to how they can stop people from doing so. He offers several ideas, including creating better relationships with consumers, putting out a better quality product, and making legal downloading more user-friendly. Cochrane is a cofounder of the AV Club and a frequent contributor.

AS YOU READ, CONSIDER THE FOLLOWING QUESTIONS:
1. Name some of the new ways cited by the author that allow people to watch movies conveniently at home.
2. According to the author, why do some people steal movies from major studios but pay to view independent films?
3. What companies does the author think are going to be the next major movie distributors?

Andy Cochrane, "Dear MPAA & RIAA: Why We Steal from You and How to Stop Us," *The AV Club Blog*, January 2008. © The AV Club Productions, Inc. Reproduced by permission.

For years now, the record and movie industries have been waging non-stop war against us, their consumers and fans. They are fighting for survival of the current business models and revenue streams, which are under an incredible assault from electronic piracy in the form of bootleg or ripped CDs and DVDs, P2P [peer-to-peer] file sharing, bittorrents, and rogue websites hosting downloads. This is a massive problem—almost every single person under the age of 50 has at some point stolen from these companies in one way or another, and they are justifiably pissed off about it. I think that they have every right to defend their copyrights and do their best to prevent the illegal free use of the products that they have paid to create, distribute, and market. I do not, however, think that they are going about it the right way. Here is my advice, which will be ignored, further cementing the demise of old media (enjoy your slow death, guys):

We steal because it is easier, not because it is cheaper, so make it easier to buy your products. Ever since iTunes made it drop-dead simple to buy new music, I find it easier to find and get a song on there than any other method (it takes [about] 1 minute and no effort). I do not buy CD's anymore because I can get them on iTunes with far less effort. That said, I hate DRM [digital rights management, a restriction on the use or copying of files], the crippled iTunes tracks makes it very hard for me to move and listen to my purchases on the 3 computers I use constantly. I know many people buy songs legally, then steal a copy of the same songs on a P2P site just so they don't have to deal with the DRM. This doesn't just apply to music—many people don't like going to the movie theater, waiting a day for Netflix to arrive, or going to a store to rent a movie—we'd much rather watch it right now. With Apple's new "rentals," Netflix's "watch now" online feature, and On Demand offerings, it is becoming easier to legally pay to watch a movie at home at your convenience than it is to steal it online or rip a DVD. Take notice of this trend, and capitalize upon it. Make it so that we can quickly, reliably, and easily access

FAST FACT

Napster, which started in June 1999, was the first hugely popular music file-sharing service. It was shut down by court order in 2001.

Top Twenty Illegally Downloaded Albums, Week of March 30, 2008

Rank	Artist	Album	Downloads
1	Moby	*Last Night*	33,284
2	Various	*Once* Soundtrack	31,356
3	Michael Jackson	*Thriller*	29,676
4	Amy Winehouse	*Back To Black*	27,485
5	Duffy	*Rockferry*	27,094
6	Air	*Once Upon a Time*	25,948
7	Jack Johnson	*Sleep Through the Static*	21,133
8	Panic at the Disco	*Pretty Odd*	19,384
9	Terry Oldfield	*Across the Universe*	19,193
10	Nine Inch Nails	*The Limitless Potential*	15,342
11	The Arcade Fire	*Black Mirror*	11,684
12	Tricky	*Crazy Claws*	10,903
13	Muse	*Live from Wembley Stadium*	9,716
14	Arctic Monkeys	*Fluorescent Adolescent*	8,943
15	Jackson Browne	*Solo Acoustic Vol. 2*	5,153
16	Various	*Juno* Soundtrack	4,432
17	Nick Cave and the Bad Seeds	*The Abattoir Blues Tour*	3,953
18	Herbie Hancock	*River: The Joni Letters*	3,013
19	Rick Ross	*Trilla*	1,932
20	The Box Tops	*The Letter*	1,103

Taken from: iDownload Chart, March 30, 2008.

your product—anywhere, anytime. Focus on finding ways to make it much, much easier to pay you than to rob you. Believe me, we don't enjoy installing software, setting up configurations, troubleshooting, and finding what we want online. We are lazy, not cheap.

We don't like paying for crap, so stop making it. I have never regretted a single dime paid for a good film or album. But I did stop going to the movies because I was sick of being bilked out of $12 every time I went out, and I pretty much never buy an entire album anymore. We hate dropping money and time on your products, only to discover that they don't just fail to meet their own hype—they often are *only* hype. I realize that you are a business, and as such a pretty basic requirement is that you need to make money. But it is time you realized that your product is entertainment, and you are not delivering good product anymore. Stop thinking of money first and product second—swap the formula around and the profit will come in droves. There is a reason that there is no "Citizen Kane II: Return of the Kane"—your predecessors knew that quality stories came first, and if a film made money it didn't necessarily need to be turned into a franchise. Instead of *Transformers 2*, or *American Idol 27*, can we please have new, exciting, interesting films and music? Don't you remember why you got into the business in the first place? Didn't you once love movies and music? Don't you want to make the next great American Film or Album? Stop chasing our money, start chasing our interests.

Never wage war on your own customers it's mean. Part of stopping us from stealing from you is going to have to involve you not being dicks about it. If you didn't come across as greedy, ignorant, evil Luddites [an opponent of technological progress], I think more people would

Bootleg CDs and DVDs have become a big business, and record labels are seeking ways to protect their copyrights without alienating their customers.

have a problem stealing your hard work. I know many people that would not blink at downloading the latest *Spiderman* movie, but who will go out of their way to pay for a copy of an indie film. Why? Because we don't like being thieves, we never have; but we don't feel like you matter—you are faceless, lawsuit-happy conglomerates of evil intentions, and as such, stealing just doesn't seem like stealing when it's against you. I have never, not once, stolen a movie—in DVD form or otherwise. I am deeply, deeply insulted that you call me a criminal with your condescending anti piracy commercials before watching the film that I just paid to see. Screw you. If you really want to win this one, you need to change your image. We are not in the right on this point—we are very, very much in the wrong, but if you want to stop us, work on being lovable, it will make the fight easier.

Recognize that there will always be piracy, and accept that fact; put the needs of the many above your fears of the few. Instead of making it hard for everyone to get and consume your product because some people steal from you, focus on making it so that anyone who wants to pay you can do so more easily. Abolish DRM (you already are starting to; kudos; now do it all the way), those who want to break it can, and those who don't want to break it still have to, just to watch the movies they bought from you on their iPods, or listen to the songs they "own" anywhere they want to (you and I both know that nobody actually owns the music or movies, it's just a limited license to enjoy it, isn't it!). You cannot win your war on piracy any more than the U.S. will win against drugs or terror, internalize that, learn to accept piracy as a given, and start to deal with it realistically. You can reduce it so much that those who steal are numerically insignificant, but not by making your product annoying to access for everyone. There are still real life pirates sailing the seas of the world, but they are nowhere near the numbers they used to be. Take realistic precautions and legal action against those who steal from you as a defensive strategy, but don't make that [your] entire focus.

Look around you and take stock of what is happening. You have the technology now to give us any song or video in the world, almost instantly, at extremely high quality. On demand is amazing, Netflix, Google, and Apple are going to be the next major movie distributors (you thought you guys were going to keep control of that one didn't you?), and there are unsigned artists outselling your talent and keeping the profit all for themselves. The iPhone deal was rejected by every carrier in the US except for AT&T mainly because they were desperate. Now look how that turned out. Apple demanded a change in the way phone manufacturers and service providers share profits, and in the process created one of the most impressive subscriber increases in the history of phone companies. Innovation is scary, but necessary. If you continue to sit on your crumbling fortress walls much longer, we won't invite you to the next big party, then what will you do? Probably blame piracy for sinking your ship. Too bad, you could have won this thing.

EVALUATING THE AUTHOR'S ARGUMENTS:

The author uses an informal, conversational tone in this viewpoint. How does that help his argument? How does it hurt it? Do you feel that his arguments will convince entertainment industry executives? Why or why not?

Lawsuits Are the Best Way to Stop Illegal Downloading

"Without the threat of consequences, far too many people were just not changing their behavior."

Recording Industry Association of America

The Recording Industry Association of America (RIAA), the umbrella organization that represents the interests of record labels and producers, has created some controversy by suing college students for illegal file sharing. In the following selection, the RIAA offers its view on this practice, giving the reasons why the organization takes the stance it does. According to the RIAA, lawsuits were not the first choice but became necessary after music fans consistently refused to obey copyright rules. Illegally downloading or sharing music, argues the RIAA, is akin to shoplifting. In both cases, it is stealing, and those who steal should face legal consequences.

AS YOU READ, CONSIDER THE FOLLOWING QUESTIONS:
1. According to the article, how many U.S. jobs are lost per year due to global music piracy?
2. What legal downloading alternatives does the author say the industry is promoting?
3. According to the article, what percentage of college students frequently download music and movies illegally from unlicensed peer-to-peer (P2P) networks?

"For Students Doing Reports," RIAA.com. Reproduced by permission.

What exactly does the RIAA do? Who does the organization represent?

The RIAA is an organization committed to helping the music business thrive. Our goal is to foster a business and legal climate that protects the ability of our members—the record companies that create, manufacture and/or distribute some 90 percent of all legitimate sound recordings produced and sold in the United States—to invest in the next generation of music.

In support of this mission, we work to protect intellectual property rights worldwide and the First Amendment rights of artists; conduct consumer, industry and technical research; and monitor and review state and federal laws, regulations and policies. We also certify Gold, Platinum, Multi-Platinum™, and Diamond sales awards, as well as Los Premios De Oro y Platino™, an award celebrating Latin music sales.

What is the RIAA's official stance on digital music piracy?

Plain and simple: piracy is bad news. While the term is commonly used, "piracy" doesn't even begin to describe what is taking place. When you go online and download songs without permission, you are stealing. The illegal downloading of music is just as wrong as shoplifting from a local convenience store—and the impact on those who create music and bring it to fans is equally devastating. For every artist you can name at the top of the Billboard music charts, there is a long line of songwriters, sound engineers, and label employees who help create those hits. They all feel the pain of music theft.

The law is quite clear here, and frankly, legal downloading is easy and doesn't cost much. Record companies have licensed hundreds of digital partners offering download and subscription services, cable and satellite radio services, Internet radio webcasting, legitimate peer-to-peer (P2P) services, video-on-demand, podcasts, CD kiosks and digital jukeboxes, mobile products such as ringbacks, ringtunes, wallpapers, audio and video downloads and more.

What Piracy Costs

How much money does the recording industry lose from piracy?

There are two categories to consider here: losses from street piracy—the manufacture and sale of counterfeit CDs—and losses from online piracy.

Bootleg CD and DVDs are displayed for sale in Ukraine. The RIAA estimates that $12.5 billion dollars is lost worldwide per year to music piracy.

One credible analysis by the Institute for Policy Innovation concludes that global music piracy causes $12.5 billion of economic losses every year, 71,060 U.S. jobs lost, a loss of $2.7 billion in workers' earnings, and a loss of $422 million in tax revenues, $291 million in personal income tax and $131 million in lost corporate income and production taxes. . . .

As you can imagine, calculating losses for online piracy is a difficult task. We do know that the pirate marketplace currently far dwarfs the legal marketplace, and when that happens, that means investment in new music is compromised.

All the same, it's important to note that across the board, piracy is a very real threat to the livelihoods of not only artists and record label employees but also thousands of less celebrated people in the music industry—from sound engineers and technicians to warehouse workers and record store clerks. Piracy undermines the future of music by depriving the industry of the resources it needs to find and develop new talent and drains millions of dollars in tax revenue from local communities and their residents.

Why Lawsuits?

What kind of message are you trying to send with your lawsuits against individuals? What do you hope to accomplish?

The ultimate goal with all our anti-piracy efforts is to protect the ability of the recording industry to invest in new bands and new music and to give legal online services a chance to flourish. That's why we educate. That's why record companies license music to legal services. And that's why, when necessary, we enforce our rights through the legal system.

FAST FACT

In December 2007 the RIAA sent out "pre-litigation settlement" letters to students at twenty-two universities as part of an ongoing campaign against online music theft.

Just as we must hold accountable the businesses that encourage theft online, individuals who engage in illegal downloading must also know there are consequences to their actions. If you violate the law and steal from record companies, musicians, songwriters and everyone else involved in making music, you can be held accountable.

With so many great legal music options available, there is really no excuse for music theft. Fans have a choice: pay a little now or a lot more later.

Don't you think some people are always going to download music illegally, no matter how many people get sued?

Of course. We're realistic. As an industry, we have lived with street piracy for years. Similarly, there will always be a degree of piracy on the Internet. It's not realistic to wipe it out entirely but instead to bring it to a level of manageable control so a legitimate marketplace can really flourish.

Lawsuits are just one piece of our overall effort to discourage illegal downloading and encourage fans to turn to legal music alternatives. Yes, we enforce our rights against people who steal music. We also work hard to educate consumers about the law and about the many legal ways to get music online. Because we know the best way to beat piracy is to offer fans a compelling legal alternative, record companies are aggressively licensing music to a great many services—from download and subscription models to Internet radio to legitimate P2P and more. Giving these legal online services a chance to flourish is a driving factor in almost everything we do.

Do you feel that it is fair to file lawsuits against downloaders? Why or Why not?

Suing individuals was by no means our first choice. Unfortunately, without the threat of consequences, far too many people were just not changing their behavior. Education alone was not enough to stem the extraordinary growth of illegal P2P use. While we have been filing lawsuits against individuals since September 2003, our first preference continues to be targeting the businesses that encourage and profit from theft. That said, it is critical that we simultaneously send a message to individuals that engaging in the theft of music is illegal.

If a store owner catches someone shoplifting merchandise, you can bet that owner takes action—just as he or she should. Our lawsuits against individuals engaged in music theft are no different. Illegal downloading is not a victimless crime: thousands of record label employees have been laid off, hundreds of artists have been cut from

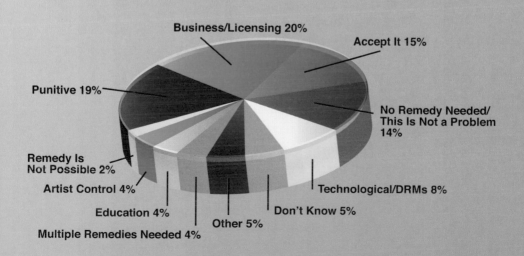

Musicians and Songwriters Speak Out on Ways to Solve the Problem of File Sharing

Business/Licensing 20%
Accept It 15%
Punitive 19%
No Remedy Needed/ This Is Not a Problem 14%
Remedy Is Not Possible 2%
Artist Control 4%
Technological/DRMs 8%
Education 4%
Don't Know 5%
Other 5%
Multiple Remedies Needed 4%

Taken from: "Artists, Musicians and the Internet," Pew Internet and American Life Project, December 5, 2004.

label rosters, numerous record stores are closing throughout the country, and due to declining sales, record companies are finding their ability to invest in new artists at risk.

With so many great legal ways to enjoy music online, there's no excuse for downloading music illegally. That's why we will continue to take a tough line against people who steal music. It's theft, it's illegal and there can be real consequences. Legal downloading doesn't cost much. Every fan has a choice: pay a little now or a lot more later.

Who Will Be Sued?

Why are only select people being sued and how are they selected?

When you log onto a P2P network, your P2P software has a default setting that automatically informs the network of your user name and the names and sizes of the files on your hard drive that are available for copying. Because all this information is publicly available to anyone on the network, it's relatively easy to look for—and find—users who are offering to "share" copyrighted music files. The networks could not work if this were not the case. Given the huge number of P2P users, we use software to search the network for infringing files, similar to the way other users search the network.

When we file a "John Doe" lawsuit against an individual engaged in illegal file sharing, we have no personal information about that individual. The complaint is filed against the Internet account holder, who is anonymous to us at the time. So anyone—and everyone— engaged in music theft is at risk for a lawsuit.

Bottom line: The best way to avoid "being caught" is to abide by the law. With all the exciting legal options available to fans, there are plenty of easy, affordable ways to get music online and do so legally.

The RIAA and College Students

Why has the RIAA chosen to specifically pursue university students?

First of all, it's important to remember that anyone engaged in music theft is at risk for a lawsuit.

That said, the piracy habits of college students remain especially and disproportionately problematic—despite real progress by the music industry on other fronts. According to some recent surveys, more than half of the nation's college students frequently download music and movies illegally from unlicensed P2P networks. That's a statistic we just cannot ignore.

As a result, we have stepped up our efforts to address college piracy across the board by significantly expanding our deterrence and education programs, continuing our push for legal music offerings on campuses, and advocating technological measures that block or curb piracy on college networks.

We know that college students are some of the most avid music fans. That's great news. The music habits and customs they develop now are likely to stay with students for life. Therefore it's especially important for us to educate them about the law; the harm suffered by musicians, labels and retailers alike when music is stolen; and the great legal ways to enjoy music online. Like students, we are huge fans of music and want to see a music community capable of developing exciting new bands.

EVALUATING THE AUTHOR'S ARGUMENTS:

The author uses a question-and-answer format to present its argument. Do you think this is an effective technique? Does the format make the article more or less persuasive? Why or why not?

Viewpoint

4

Lawsuits Are the Wrong Way to Stop Illegal Downloading

John Gruenfelder

"Rather than put all this time and effort into suing potential customers, it sure would be nice if the music industry could offer a system that everybody liked."

In the following article author John Gruenfelder details the ways the Recording Industry Association of America (RIAA) targets college students suspected of illegally sharing copyrighted music files. He admits that file sharing is widespread on campus but disagrees with the methods the RIAA has been using to combat the practice. He argues that its lawsuits resemble extortion more than a reasonable effort to stop file sharing. Such tactics do not solve the problems and only serve to alienate potential customers, he writes. Gruenfelder is a columnist for the *Massachusetts Daily Collegian*, the student newspaper of the University of Massachusetts.

AS YOU READ, CONSIDER THE FOLLOWING QUESTIONS:

1. According to the article, what university had the sixth-highest number of file sharers in the country?

John Gruenfelder, "Not the Right Way, RIAA," *The Daily Collegian*, March 5, 2007. © 2007 *The Daily Collegian*. Reproduced by permission.

2. According to the author, what is a typical fee for pre-lawsuit settlements offered by the RIAA?
3. What point does Gruenfelder make about the cost of downloaded music as compared to that of a CD?

The good people at the Recording Industry Association of America (RIAA) are redoubling their efforts against college students. As a recent article in the *Massachusetts Daily Collegian* described, the RIAA has launched a new lawsuit and awareness campaign aimed at stopping college students from illegally sharing copyrighted music files via campus networks.

It's no secret that file-sharing is widespread on campuses. A recent report released by the Associated Press even indicated that the University of Massachusetts has the 6th highest number of file sharers in the country. This sort of activity is, of course, illegal, and yet the means by which the RIAA attempts to combat this problem are nothing short of criminal themselves.

The RIAA's chief tactic is to search for file sharers on the Internet and, once identified, sue them for copyright infringement. "Identified" is used rather loosely here, however, [as] most of these lawsuits are filed against John Does [users of a particular Internet service provider (ISP) who have yet to be identified] pending some actual form of personal identification. Relatively few of these cases actually go to trial because, once identified, many people choose to settle out of court. There are many reasons why an accused person might do this even when innocent, the primary one being that the RIAA's settlement amount is lower than what attorney fees might be.

Pre-Lawsuit Settlement Letters

The RIAA's latest college push has a new twist to it: pre-lawsuit settlement letters. That's right; the RIAA will now kindly inform you via letter that you may settle for a "discounted rate before a lawsuit is ever filed." Not only that, but thanks to the RIAA's new Web site, www .p2plawsuits.com, you can admit guilt and pay your settlement fee with a major credit card all from the comfort of home. Thirty-seven

Brad Buckles, executive vice president for antipiracy in the RIAA, speaks at a press conference about the association's efforts to combat downloading piracy by suing file-sharing students.

UMass Amherst students will be receiving these letters in the first wave of the new campaign.

Oh, happy day. I'm not sure what to call this other than extortion. The RIAA promises not to drag you through a lawsuit if you'll hand over a fee (typically on the order of $3,000–$5,000). No wonder the RIAA is often referred to on the Internet as the "Mafia."

As recent court proceedings have shown in *UMG v. Lindor*, one of the few cases which has gone to trial, the RIAA's evidence often borders on the laughable. Since these cases so rarely go to trial, one would assume that the RIAA would make every effort to win, yet the evidence presented from the third parties they contract to find file sharers (companies like MediaSentry) and even their own expert witness shows that very little time goes into tracking down the accused. It is often done automatically by software.

Here at UMass, the Office of Information Technology [OIT] receives a steady stream of copyright infringement notices which require a student's network connection be shutoff. They receive as many as 40 per day and almost all from the RIAA. The evidence provided to OIT is similar to that which the RIAA has presented in court, but as they receive so many complaints, OIT is unable to independently verify the claims. This new RIAA campaign would seem to indicate that some of these notices will be giving way to pre-lawsuit letters.

Fees Are "Devastating" to Students

Defending the lawsuit or paying the fee, either one would be devastating to most college students. It's important, therefore, to have an idea of what to do if you are innocent and happen to fall into the RIAA's cross hairs. Regardless of how it ends, you'll be paying money to somebody, so get yourself a lawyer and hope the final resolution doesn't take too long. Being informed is important since the RIAA's detection methods can point the finger at the wrong person and have done so on numerous occasions. Once you've been sued [your] only recourse is to prove your innocence and that's a very sad way to conduct justice. If you are engaged in illegally sharing copyrighted files, the best course of action is clearly to stop. But even if you're not, that's no guarantee that the RIAA won't come knocking.

Rather than put all this time and effort into suing potential customers, it sure would be nice if the music industry could offer a system that everybody liked. For starters, no more encumbering digital rights management (DRM) on music, so that you can use the files with any portable

FAST FACT

In 2003 the RIAA settled a lawsuit against a twelve-year-old girl. She was ordered to pay two thousand dollars.

player. And lower prices. One dollar per song is not particularly high, yet it also seems reasonable that the cost of a downloaded CD's worth of music should cost substantially less than a physically manufactured CD, which it does not.

UMass students can get music from Ruckus [an ad-supported online music service] for free, but even that system has substantial flaws. You can only use Ruckus if you're running Windows, and all music includes Microsoft's DRM so you can only use it on portable players which support it. Unfortunately, that list of players does not include iPods, which are by far the most prevalent.

Whichever route the new RIAA strategy takes, it's going to end up hurting a lot of students—some guilty, some innocent. And these tactics will continue to create ill feelings towards the music industry. If I was trying to build a new online market, that's the last thing I would want.

EVALUATING THE AUTHOR'S ARGUMENTS:

Compare this viewpoint with the previous one from the Recording Industry Association of America (RIAA). Which one do you feel presented a more convincing argument? Why?

Social Networking Sites Should Pay Royalties to Artists

Billy Bragg

"Both the corporations and the kids, it seems, want the use of our music without having to pay for it."

Author Billy Bragg was inspired to write the following piece after hearing that the founder of a British social networking site had sold his shares for $600 million. Bragg argues that since the business has reaped large financial rewards, musicians who have provided content for the site should share in those rewards. He discounts the claim that networking sites pay musicians in free publicity; he notes that radio stations also provide publicity, but they still pay royalties to artists. As technology continues to change, he writes, new ground rules have to be established. Bragg is a noted songwriter, musician, and activist.

AS YOU READ, CONSIDER THE FOLLOWING QUESTIONS:

1. According to Bragg, what was the membership of Bebo.com after just two years?

2. According to Bragg, what did Bebo cofounder Michael Birch say regarding the relationship he wanted Bebo to have with artists?
3. According to the author, what is the first legal agreement some new musicians will enter into?

L ast week [March 2008] at South by Southwest, the rock music conference held every year in Austin, Tex., the talk in hotel lobbies, coffeeshops and the convention center was dominated by one issue: how do musicians make a living in the age of the Internet? It's a problem our industry has struggled with in the wake of the rising popularity of sharing mp3 music files.

Our discussions were brought into sharp relief when news reached Austin of the sale of Bebo.com to AOL for a staggering $850 million. Bebo is a social-networking site whose membership has risen to 40 million in just two years. In Britain, it ranks with MySpace and Facebook in popularity, although its users tend to come from a younger age group.

Estimates suggested that the founder, Michael Birch (along with his wife and co-founder, Xochi), walked away with $600 million for his 70 percent stake in the company.

I heard the news with a particular piquancy, as Mr. Birch has cited me as an influence in Bebo's attitude toward artists. He got in touch two years ago after I took MySpace to task over its proprietary rights clause. I was concerned that the site was harvesting residual rights from original songs posted there by unsigned musicians. As a result of my complaints, MySpace changed its terms and conditions to state clearly that all rights to material appearing on the site remain with the originator.

A few weeks later, Mr. Birch came to see me at my home. He was hoping to expand his business by hosting music and wanted my advice on how to construct an artist-centered environment where musicians could post original songs without fear of losing control over their work. Following our talks, Mr. Birch told the press that he wanted Bebo to be a site that worked for artists and held their interests first and foremost.

Should Royalties Be Paid to Artists?

In our discussions, we largely ignored the elephant in the room: the issue of whether he ought to consider paying some kind of royalties to the artists. After all, wasn't he using their music to draw members—and advertising—to his business? Social-networking sites like Bebo argue that they have no money to distribute—their value is their membership.

Time Spent by Britons Monthly on Social Networking Sites

Rank	Social Network	Time per Person
1	Second Life	5hrs 29ms
2	Habbo	3hs 06ms
3	Tagged	2hs 40ms
4	Facebook	2hs 32ms
5	Bebo	2hs 15ms
6	MySpace	1h 25ms
7	FaceParty	1h 05ms
8	Netlog	50ms
9	Orkut	48ms
10	LinkedIn	43ms

Taken from: Nielsen/NetRatings, September 25, 2007.

Billy Bragg is an accomplished musician and songwriter who believes that social networking sites like MySpace and Bebo should pay artists royalties because they are making money off artists' efforts without paying for them.

Well, last week Michael Birch realized the value of his membership. I'm sure he'll be rewarding those technicians and accountants who helped him achieve this success. Perhaps he should also consider the contribution of his artists.

The musicians who posted their work on Bebo.com are no different from investors in a start-up enterprise. Their investment is the content provided for free while the site has no liquid assets. Now that the business has reaped huge benefits, surely they deserve a dividend.

What's at stake here is more than just the morality of the market. The huge social-networking sites that seek to use music as free content are as much to blame for the malaise currently affecting the industry as the music lover who downloads songs for free. Both the corporations and the kids, it seems, want the use of our music without having to pay for it.

Royalty Rules Should Apply to the Internet, Too

The claim that sites such as MySpace and Bebo are doing us a favor by promoting our work is disingenuous. Radio stations also promote our work, but they pay us a royalty that recognizes our contribution to their business. Why should that not apply to the Internet, too?

Technology is advancing far too quickly for the old safeguards of intellectual property rights to keep up, and while we wait for the technical fixes to emerge, those of us who want to explore the opportunities the Internet offers need to establish a set of ground rules that give us the power to decide how our music is exploited and by whom.

We need to do this not for the established artists who already have lawyers, managers and careers, but for the fledgling songwriters and musicians posting original material onto the Web tonight. The first legal agreement that they enter into as artists will occur when they click to accept the terms and conditions of the site that will host their music. Worryingly, no one is looking out for them.

If young musicians are to have a chance of enjoying a fruitful career, then we need to establish the principle of artists' rights throughout the Internet—and we need to do it now.

EVALUATING THE AUTHOR'S ARGUMENTS:

The author has a personal involvement with this story, both as a musician and as someone who was in early talks with Bebo on how to involve musicians. How do these credentials strengthen or weaken his argument?

Social Networking Sites Should Not Pay Royalties to Artists

Geoff Taylor

"[The record labels'] mission is to turn more of the growing number of streams, copies and downloads into pounds and pence to share across the value chain."

The following viewpoint is a response to the widening popularity of musicians' online presence and these artists' use of alternative models of generating revenue. Geoff Taylor contends that the most secure way to ensure an artist's success, both to begin selling in the music industry and to stay selling in the music industry, there is no other way to generate revenue other than the traditional methods of record labels. This, according to the author, would include social networking sites or other online endeavors that would pay artists for their music. Taylor believes the Internet should be used as another landscape for record labels to effectively monetize on behalf of the benefit of artists. Geoff Taylor is the chief executive of the BPI (formerly known as British Phonographic

Industry), an organization that represents the British recorded music business.

AS YOU READ, CONSIDER THE FOLLOWING QUESTIONS:
1. According to the author, why would "new distribution models" only work successfully when artists like Madonna or Prince use them?
2. According to the author, why have the services that record labels offer to an artist become more important?
3. What other capabilities does the author present that he believes are "essential" for an artist? Why are these capabilities so important for the artist?

There is no doubt that the recording industry is going through a period of unprecedented change. The very foundation upon which our business is built—the ability to generate income from the artists of today to invest in the artists of tomorrow—is being threatened by widespread copyright theft.

There Is No Alternative to Traditional Record Label Business

Operations such as that against the illegal OiNK service represent just one part of how our industry is successfully managing the challenges of the digital age. There is no magic bullet to eradicate copyright theft and no single anti-piracy action or business model will change the world. Even so, our mission is to turn more of the growing number of streams, copies and downloads into pounds and pence to share across the value chain.

FAST FACT

According to MySpace, the top music genre on its site is hip-hop, with over 2.5 million acts onboard.

Some have suggested that a larger issue for industry is the ability of artists such as Radiohead to seek alternative distribution channels. But there is in fact nothing

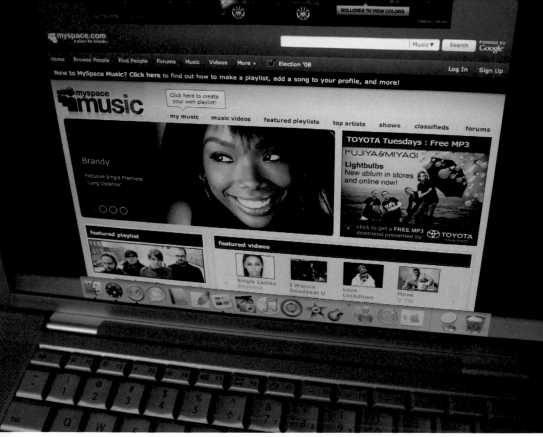

The author argues that social networking sites like MySpace should not pay artists royalties because they help promote the artists' music.

new in established artists setting up their own record label—Prince, Simply Red, Oasis, The Beatles, and Led Zeppelin have done the same thing in the past.

But what the new distribution models recently adopted by the Charlatans, Madonna, Prince and others have in common is that they generate revenue streams that are far less vulnerable to copyright theft: with recordings being used to drive the sales of concert tickets in the case of Madonna, or as a promotional vehicle to claim a share of newspaper income in the case of Prince. And models such as these are only practical for well-known artists who have built up large fanbases after years of marketing and investment by record labels.

The bottom line is that no-one is offering an alternative to the core business model of a record label—investing in unknown artists on the basis that they will generate income in the future. To cover their investments in new music, record labels are seeking to earn income from a wider range of artists' revenue streams.

Lines are blurring between the traditional record label and other music companies. While opportunities arise for others to enter the record business, record labels are developing broader business models to generate income from revenue streams outside recorded music.

Record Labels Offer Much More to Artists

The many services that a record label offers to an artist have become more important as media channels proliferate. In addition to their traditional expertise in international physical distribution and marketing, labels have networks of relationships to collect licensing income globally to remunerate artists, music publishers and other rightsholders.

The back catalogues and broad portfolios of larger record companies give them negotiating power in striking deals that can benefit all the artists on their roster, while digital channels are opening up many new opportunities to promote acts across a multiplicity of online

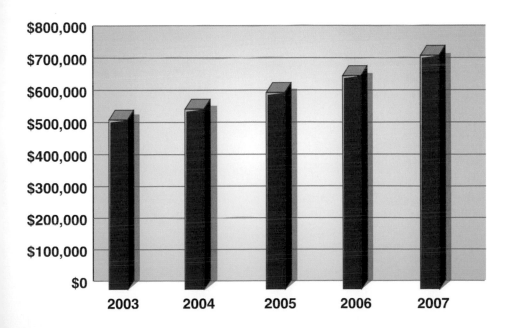

Royalties Paid by Broadcast Music Inc. (BMI) to Songwriters, Composers, and Music Publishers

Taken from: BMI, September 4, 2007.

channels and exploit catalogue more effectively than has been possible through physical retail.

Labels are also well-placed to generate new income from brand partnerships and synchronisation. These capabilities are essential for artists trying to build a long-term career.

The Online World Must Work Together with Record Labels

The BPI is at the forefront of the industry's efforts to ensure that there is a fair financial return for artists and those who invest in creating new music. We believe the prevalent culture of online copyright theft will be curbed through a combination of consumer education, new business models, more robust action by ISPs against online copyright theft and stricter enforcement by industry and government.

We believe that the internet will become an environment in which creativity can be effectively monetised, as our society, economy and culture has too much to lose if we do not ensure that creators are rewarded.

We do not need to convince anyone of the emotional value of the music they love, but if the record industry is to reach its potential online, we must succeed in our mission to convince new industry partners, policy makers and consumers that an online and mobile ecosystem in which music is respected and valued is in the interest of everyone.

EVALUATING THE AUTHOR'S ARGUMENTS:

The author is an executive officer for an organization that supports record labels. How do you think his position influences his argument? What are the author's major points?

Webcasters Need to Pay Fair Royalties

John Simson

"Those who are profiting from playing . . . music need to pay fair and reasonable rates."

In the following viewpoint John Simson argues that Internet radio stations, also called Webcasters, need to pay fair royalty rates. The author traces the short history of Internet royalty rate battles and the creation of the Copyright Royalty Board (CRB), a group formed to set fair rates. Thus far, the CRB has not found a solution acceptable to both Webcasters and artists' representatives. Simson writes that efforts at fairness have been hindered because large Webcasters have formed lobbying groups under the guise of trying to help small Webcasters, when in fact they are just representing their own corporate interests. Simson is the executive director of SoundExchange, an organization that collects and distributes royalties on behalf of the recording industry.

AS YOU READ, CONSIDER THE FOLLOWING QUESTIONS:
1. Who makes up the Copyright Royalty Board (CRB)?
2. Name three large corporations who are in the Webcasting business.
3. According to the author, under CRB terms, how much would a Webcaster pay per month in royalties for a consumer who listens forty hours per month?

There's a lot of commotion in Washington these days over Internet radio royalty rates. Much of it is coming from large corporate Webcasters and their lobbyists, who are trying to execute a classic Washington end-run. They don't like the results they got from a process they set in motion, so they have gone back to Congress with sky-is-falling histrionics in hopes of getting a do-over.

They're hiding behind a coalition that portrays itself as being a grassroots movement made up of small, independent Webcasters, when in fact large corporate Webcasters funded the coalition and are calling the shots.

The issue? Fair and reasonable royalty rates to compensate performers and record labels when their music is played via Webcasting (also referred to as Internet radio) and on satellite radio and cable audio music channels.

The Background

Some quick background: A few years ago, legislators set out to strike a balance between the rights of artists and labels to be fairly compensated for their work and the needs of Webcasters and satellite services to obtain licenses for massive quantities of music. To do that, Congress established a system to set royalty rates for music played via digital technology. Every recording protected under U.S. law could be used by a service, provided that service abided by the terms of the license and paid rates set by a panel of arbitrators and approved by the Librarian of Congress.

FAST FACT

In July 2008 free Internet radio station Last.fm announced that it would begin compensating unsigned artists with a percentage of ad revenue.

After the first Webcasting proceeding ended in 2002, Webcasters claimed that the process cost too much and yielded unfairly high rates, so they successfully lobbied Congress to set up an impartial panel to set rates. This resulted in the creation of the Copyright Royalty Board (CRB), comprised of three impartial expert judges.

The CRB convened an 18-month review that involved weeks of live hearings. Judges heard from dozen of witnesses, took countless depositions, and read tens of thousands of pages of evidence from all interested parties. The judges were privy to confidential proprietary information about the revenues and costs of large and small Webcasters, commercial and noncommercial services, the financial details of performers and record labels large and small, and private deals that had been negotiated between Webcasters and record companies.

Webcasters Balk at the New Rules

In short, the CRB did what Congress asked it to do, at the behest of Webcasters. But when the CRB set what it judged to be fair and reasonable royalty rates, the Webcasters decided they were too high, cried foul and denounced the very process they had sought.

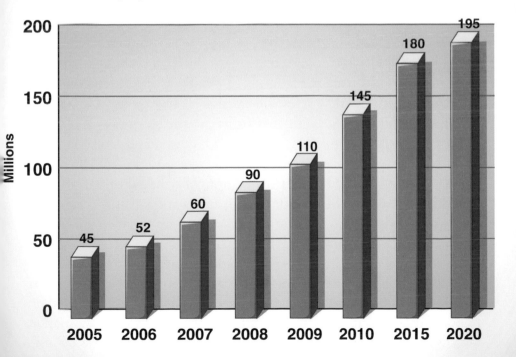

Actual and Projected Internet Radio Listeners

This graph shows actual numbers of Internet radio listeners through 2007 and projected numbers for 2009 and beyond.

Taken from: Bridge Ratings, April 25, 2007.

Independent Internet radio stations successfully lobbied Congress to create the Copyright Royalty Board in 2002.

Large corporations like Time Warner's AOL, Microsoft, Yahoo!, and Clear Channel are in the Webcasting business in a big way. But you would not know it from the coalition set up by big Webcasters to fight the CRB's decision. According to the Chicken Little–themed coalition, the industry is made up of small, independent business Webcasters, and the new rates will cause Webcasting to "die."

While nothing could be further from the truth, a bill was recently introduced by Representatives Jay Inslee (D-Wash.) and Don Manzullo (R-Ill.) that would drastically cut the royalty rates and provide large commercial Webcasters with an estimated annual windfall of $10 million or more that would otherwise be paid to artists and labels. Comparable legislation was introduced in the Senate May 10 [2007] by Ron Wyden (D-Ore.) and Sam Brownback (R-Kan.).

If the intent of the Inslee and Manzullo bill was truly to help small Webcasters, a bill to push forward the Small Webcaster Settlement Act of 2003 would have accomplished that. In 2003, Congress decided on policy grounds that small Webcasters should receive a below-market rate, given the infancy of the medium.

Those Who Profit from Music Should Pay the Musicians

Viable, financially profitable Webcasters seem to feel they should be able to play music and make a healthy profit without fairly compensating performers and record labels. The nonprofit group of which I am executive director, SoundExchange, collects and distributes royalties due artists and labels when their music is Webcast and serves as an advocate for these hard-working individuals who far too often are being left out of the equation.

After all, what we're talking about here is music Webcasting, where businesses are being built around a sole product: music. Those who are profiting from playing that music need to pay fair and reasonable rates, which is what the CRB set out to accomplish, and achieved.

To put the whole matter in context consider that, under terms of the CRB decision, a consumer who listens 40 hours a month to one Webcaster will cost the Webcaster only 68 cents a month in royalties in 2007—a sum far less than most Webcasters charge listeners for subscriptions.

A pretty fundamental premise for running a business is that if you make a product, you sell it for whatever price you wish and keep the profits— but if you don't make the product, you sell it only if you pay a reasonable fee to those who did make it. But that's a premise with which some of those in the Webcasting business don't agree, and that's why they're running to Congress to escape.

EVALUATING THE AUTHOR'S ARGUMENTS:

The author is the executive director of an organization that stands to benefit from higher Internet radio royalty rates. In your opinion, does this lessen the power of his argument, strengthen it, or have no effect?

Viewpoint

8

High Royalty Payments Will Put Webcasters Out of Business

Jon Healey

"The new royalties themselves don't sound like much . . . but they represent a stunning increase for small and non-commercial webcasters."

In the following viewpoint Jon Healey discusses the continually shifting rules on royalty rates for Webcasters and how these rules affect different Webcasters in different ways. The royalty rates are affordable for large broadcasters with large subscriber bases and advertising revenue, but, he writes, larger royalty rates could put many smaller Webcasters out of business. He cites the case of Internet radio station Live365, which could be faced with royalty rates that are higher than 100 percent of the company's revenue. The matter is further complicated because record labels do not want to put smaller Webcasters out of business as they provide sorely needed exposure for little-known independent musicians. Healey is an editoral writer for the *Los Angeles Times*.

AS YOU READ, CONSIDER THE FOLLOWING QUESTIONS:
1. How much did SoundExchange collect in Webcasting royalties in 2006, according to the article?
2. What percentage of songs heard on Internet radio are from independent labels?
3. Name three large Webcasters that are, according to the author, among SoundExchange's main targets for royalty collection.

[In June 2007], top executives from four popular online radio services sent a letter to every member of Congress, warning that new royalty rates for online radio broadcasters "will cause immediate bankruptcy of the majority of the Internet radio industry" on July 15, the day they take effect.

The new royalties themselves don't sound like much—for an all-music station, less than 1.8 cents per listener per hour this year, rising to 3 cents in 2010—but they represent a stunning increase for small and non-commercial webcasters, as well as firms offering a wide array of customized channels.

Opponents of the new rates have trotted out a number of horror stories and absurdities to challenge the copyright royalty judges' reasoning. SoundExchange, which represents labels and performers, collected about $18 million in webcasting royalties [in 2006], and a total of $53 million since 1998. But the new minimum fee of $500 per channel would force three webcasters that offer thousands of customized channels—RealNetworks, Yahoo and Pandora—to cough up $1.15 billion per year, according to attorneys for the companies.

Meanwhile, the judges' decision to charge all commercial webcasters a flat fee per song performed, with the new rates applying retroactively to last year's transmissions, spells doom for some popular stations with limited advertising sales. Pressured by Congress, SoundExchange negotiated a deal with small commercial webcasters in late 2002 that allowed them to pay as little as 10% of their gross revenue in royalties, with a minimum of $2,000 a year. Although the deal expired in 2005, small webcasters continued to pay a percentage of their revenues while waiting for new rates to be set. Mark Lam, chief executive of webcasting aggregator Live365, said a handful of

Len and Nora Peralta Webcast their radio show from their home in Lakewood, Ohio. The author argues that excessive royalties will put stations like the Peraltas' out of business.

webcasters on his network who had paid the minimum now owe tens or even hundreds of thousands of dollars in royalties for 2006 and the first half of 2007. If forced to pay, they could lose their homes, Lam said, adding, "It's unfathomable."

A Familiar Battle for Webcasters

Truth be told, "unfathomable" doesn't really apply to the webcasters' situation because they've been through this kind of drama before. In 2002, a federal panel set royalty rates for webcasters at more than 2 cents per listener per hour for commercial, Web-only stations, retroactive to 1998. Although the Librarian of Congress later cut the rate in half, many webcasters still pulled the plug because they couldn't afford to pay the fee. The online radio industry ran to Capitol Hill, persuading Congress that the expensive royalty-setting process had been unfair to small webcasters who couldn't afford to plead their case. The result was the Small Webcaster Settlement Act, which opened the door for SoundExchange to strike the percentage-of-revenue arrangement with small commercial webcasters and offer a discounted set of fees for non-commercial stations.

The basic problems here include a royalty-setting process that promotes brinkmanship. Many labels and artists, particularly the independent ones not affiliated with the Recording Industry Assn. of America, see webcasters as critical alternatives to over-the-air stations, whose shrunken playlists leave little room for new or lesser-known artists. Unlike the major-label-dominated airwaves, 30% or more of the tunes heard on Internet stations are from indies. (That estimate is based on royalties collected by SoundExchange, so it almost certainly understates the difference between over-the-air playlists and online ones because small webcasters often fail to report what they play.) Yet negotiators for the labels have been reluctant to strike discounted royalty deals with small-fry webcasters because of the precedent they could set—not just for larger webcasters, but also for satellite and cable-TV music services.

It's worth noting that two months after the Copyright Royalty Board set the new royalty rates, SoundExchange offered to extend the existing discounts for small webcasters (a move that may or may not spare the webcasters on Live365's network, depending on the limit SoundExchange places on audience size). "Artists and labels are offering a below-market rate to subsidize small webcasters because Congress has made it clear that this is a policy it desires to advance, at least for the next few years. We look at it as artists and labels doing their part to help small operators get a stronger foothold," SoundExchange executive director John Simson said.

FAST FACT

Satellite and cable radio stations pay about half the royalty rate that Internet stations are required to pay.

In a recent interview, Simson said SoundExchange has also offered to extend the discounts enjoyed by non-commercial webcasters. SoundExchange's main target is the limited number of large webcasters with strong advertising or subscriber revenues, such as AOL, Yahoo and RealNetworks. More than 80% of the royalties paid last year came from 10 webcasters, SoundExchange reported; by contrast, all small webcasters combined paid only 2% of those fees.

A Difference in Philosophies

At the same time, there's a fundamental philosophical difference between some webcasters (and their listeners), who feel they are entitled to play the songs they love online, and many in the music industry, who think webcasting should be open only to those who can afford to pay a certain level of royalties. Simson defends charging a $500 minimum even for amateurs and non-commercial webcasters, noting that fishermen and golfers spend more per year to pursue their hobbies. Ben Newhouse, editor of the online trade magazine *Royalty Week,* noted that the 2006 royalty rates amount to about $6.50 per listener per year, based on a Bridge Ratings report that the average listener consumes more than 470 hours of Internet radio annually. "Can anyone objectively state it is unreasonable for copyright owners to charge $6.49 for the right to broadcast 473.2 hours of music? $6.49 is a Happy Meal," Newhouse wrote.

Clearly, with CD sales in free fall, the music industry's longstanding interest in the promotional value of radio is giving way to its hunger for new revenue streams. Labels and artists are even pushing to collect royalties from over-the-air stations, which have long been exempted (they pay royalties only to songwriters).

Still, the industry has to be careful here because the new webcasting royalty rates would not only raise the barriers to entry but also rule out some business models. In particular, the new minimums are lethal to free webcasters such as Pandora, which use the unique capabilities of computers and the Web to match listeners with customized online channels. They improve radio programming by narrowcasting instead of broadcasting—offering multiple stations with niche appeal, rather than pitching more broadly palpable fare to the masses. Such services bring badly needed exposure to obscure genres and artists, overlooked releases and older material.

The biggest risk for the music industry is that the higher minimums and rising rates could trigger the kind of consolidation that

Changing Royalty Rates for Independent Internet Radio Broadcasters

The following chart shows old royalties versus new Copyright Royalty Board (CRB) royalties.

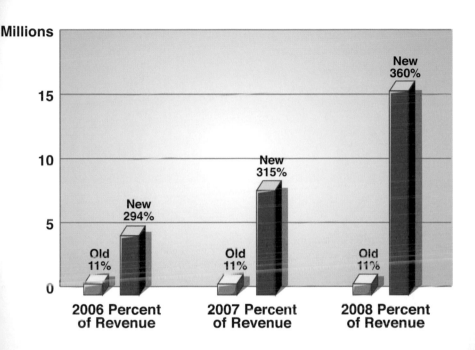

Taken from: *Radio and Internet Newsletter*, June 2007.

has made over-the-air radio a no-fly zone for all but a fraction of the tracks released on CD. Such consolidation would almost certainly reduce the diversity of music online, which runs contrary to the needs of most artists and labels as well as the public's interest. Look at Live365 as an example. According to spokesman Rod Hsiao, more than two-thirds of the songs played by the broadcasters aggregated there come from indie acts and record companies. That makes Live365 valuable to a broad swath of the music industry, even if it's not especially helpful to the major record companies whose acts dominate commercial radio. But Live365, which paid

$1.3 million in royalties last year, is looking at a revised bill of $4.7 million under the new rules. That's more than 100% of the company's radio-related revenues, Hsiao said, adding, "it would be better for us not to play music." That doesn't sound like a Happy Meal for anybody.

EVALUATING THE AUTHOR'S ARGUMENTS:

Find a particularly compelling point that the author makes. What are the aspects that make it such a strong argument? Is it a matter of compelling facts, a persuasive style, or something else?

Facts About the Music Industry

Editor's note: These facts can be used in reports or papers to reinforce or add credibility when making important points or claims.

Music Sales in 2007

- According to the RIAA, in 2007, 500.5 million albums in the form of CDs, cassettes, LPs, and other formats were purchased, down 15 percent from 2006.
- During the same period, the number of digital tracks sold rose 45 percent to 844.2 million.
- The majority of music, 82 percent, was sold as full-length albums; of those less than 1 percent was sold as vinyl LPs.
- The biggest buyers of music were people aged forty-five years and older.
- The largest percentage of music—29 percent—was sold through a store other than a record store. Twelve percent of music was sold through a record club, and about 2 percent was sold through a TV, newspaper, magazine ad, or toll-free number.
- Women bought slightly more music than men (50.8 percent vs. 49.2).

Who Gets the Money?

On a typical major-label release costing $15.99, the money is split in this way:

- 17¢ to musicians unions
- 80¢ to packaging and manufacturing
- 82¢ to publishing royalties
- 80¢ to retail profits
- 90¢ to distributions
- $1.60 to artist royalties
- $1.70 to profit for the label
- $2.40 to marketing and promotion
- $2.91 to label overhead
- $3.89 to retail overhead

Music and the Internet

- As of January 2008 there were over 8 million bands and artists on MySpace.
- Amount in U.S. dollars that MySpace paid musicians for their songs: 0.
- Eighty-seven percent of musicians report that they promote, advertise, or display their music online, and 83 percent provide free samples or previews of their music on the Internet.
- Sixty-nine percent of musicians say they sell their music online.
- On CD Baby, an online record store for independent acts, musicians make between $6 and $12 an album. Since 1998, 150,000 artists have sold over $65 million of music on the site.
- As of 2008 iTunes had sold more than 4 billion songs, which constituted 70 percent of all downloaded music sales.
- iTunes is installed on nearly 30 percent of computers worldwide.

Illegal Downloading and Lawsuits

- From 2003 to 2008 the RIAA filed twenty thousand lawsuits against people for illegally downloading music.
- The pre-litigation settlement costs for such cases are between three thousand and five thousand dollars.
- In 2008 a Bronx woman settled a case with the RIAA after she admitted to illegally downloading songs on the file-sharing site Kazaa. She was fined $6,050 for downloading eight songs, or about $756 per song. Among the artists she downloaded were the Eagles, Sade, and Lenny Kravitz.
- Amount the Copyright Act allows, per track, as a fine for illegal downloading: $150,000.
- Only one RIAA file-sharing case has gone to trial. The case involved twenty-four stolen tracks and resulted in a fine of $222,000, or $9,250 per track.

Quick Tracks

- Between radio, CDs, and music videos, the average young person listens to three to four hours of music a day.
- Teens fifteen to nineteen years old buy about 12 percent of music sold.

- The top-selling genre of music is rock.
- The five top-selling albums of all time are: 1. *Eagles, Their Greatest Hits, 1971–1975*, Eagles. 2. *Thriller*, Michael Jackson. 3. *Led Zeppelin IV*, Led Zeppelin. 4. *The Wall*, Pink Floyd. 5. *Back in Black*, AC/DC.
- Since 2005 the video game Guitar Hero has sold 20 million copies.
- The game publishers pay record labels about ten thousand dollars to re-record a song for the game and about twenty-five thousand dollars to use the original.
- Sales of the 1970s-era Aerosmith song "Same Old Song and Dance" jumped 446 percent after it appeared on Guitar Hero 3.

Organizations to Contact

The editors have compiled the following list of organizations concerned with the issues debated in this book. The descriptions are derived from materials provided by the organizations. All have publications or information available for interested readers. The list was compiled on the date of publication of the present volume; the information provided here may change. Be aware that many organizations take several weeks or longer to respond to queries, so allow as much time as possible.

Alliance of Artists and Recording Companies (AARC)
700 N. Fairfax St., Ste. 601
Alexandria, VA 22314
(703) 535-8101
fax: (703) 535-8105
e-mail: contact@aarcroyalties.com
Web site: http://aarcroyalties.com

AARC is a nonprofit organization representing featured artists and recording companies, in the areas of home taping/private copy royalties and rental royalties. AARC was formed to collect and distribute Audio Home Recording Act of 1992 (AHRA) royalties to featured recording artists and sound recording copyright owners.

**American Federation of Musicians of the
United States and Canada (AFM)**
1501 Broadway, Ste. 600
New York, NY 10036
(212) 869-1330
fax: (212) 764-6134
e-mail: presoffice@afm.org
Web site: www.afm.org

AFM represents the interests of professional musicians. The organization negotiates agreements, seeks to protect ownership of recorded music and secure benefits such as health care and pensions, and lobbies legislators. AFM publishes the magazine *International Musician*.

American Society of Composers, Authors, and Publishers (ASCAP)
1 Lincoln Plaza
New York, NY 10023
(212) 621-6000
fax: (212) 724-9064
toll-free: (800) 952-7227
e-mail: info@ascap.com
Web site: www.ascap.com

ASCAP is a membership association of more than 330,000 U.S. composers, songwriters, lyricists, and music publishers. ASCAP protects the rights of its members by licensing and distributing royalties for the nondramatic public performances of their copyrighted works. ASCAP publishes the *ASCAP Advantage*.

Electronic Frontier Foundation (EFF)
454 Shotwell St.
San Francisco, CA 94110-1914
(415) 436-9333
fax: (415) 436-9993
e-mail: information@eff.org
Web site: www.eff.org/about/contact

EFF is a small, grassroots legal advocacy nonprofit supported by member contributions. The organization specializes in cases in which it can help shape law in the areas of digital freedom, including more consumer-friendly file-sharing rules. Its Web site offers a blog with the latest news of the "electronic frontier."

Future of Music Coalition (FMC)
1615 L St. NW #520
Washington, DC 20036
(202) 822-2051
e-mail: summit@futureofmusic.org
Web site: www.futureofmusic.org

The Future of Music Coalition is a not-for-profit collaboration between members of the music, technology, public policy, and intellectual property law communities that seeks to bring together diverse voices to identify and find creative solutions to the new challenges of technology. The FMC publishes articles and generates research on the music industry. The coalition publishes the *FMC Newsletter*.

International Webcasting Association (IWA)
4206 F Technology Ct.
Chantilly, VA 20151
e-mail: info@webcasters.org
Web site: www.webcasters.org

The IWA is the largest worldwide nonprofit trade organization dedicated to the growth and development of Webcasting and streaming media over the Internet and other networks. The IWA offers its members networking, information, and business assistance. The organization publishes the *IWA News*.

Just Plain Folks Songwriting/Musician Networking Organization
5327 Kit Dr.
Indianapolis, IN 46237
e-mail: justplainfolks@aol.com
Web site: www.jpfolks.com

Just Plain Folks is a networking group for people in the music industry, including musicians, journalists, and retailers. The organization facilitates online networking as well as face-to-face meetings. Its Web site offers a member database, blog, and news about the music industry.

National Music Publishers' Association (NMPA)
101 Constitution Ave. NW, Ste. 705 E
Washington, DC 20001
(202) 742-4375
fax: (202) 742-4377
e-mail: pr@nmpa.org
Web site: www.nmpa.org

The NMPA is the largest U.S. music publishing trade association. It represents its members to protect their property rights on the legislative, litigation, and regulatory fronts. NMPA publishes the newsletter *NMPA News and Views*.

The Recording Academy
3402 Pico Blvd.
Santa Monica, CA 90405
(310) 392-3777
fax: (310) 399-3090
e-mail: memservices@grammy.com
Web site: www.grammy.com

The Recording Academy's mission is "to positively impact the lives of musicians, industry members and our society at large." The group's work focuses on advocacy, music education, and philanthropy. The Recording Academy is also known for presenting the Grammy Awards. The group publishes *Grammy* magazine.

Recording Industry Association of America (RIAA)
1025 F St. NW, 10th Floor
Washington, DC 20004
(202) 775-0101
Web site: www.riaa.com

The RIAA is the trade group that represents the U.S. recording industry. The organization protects the intellectual property rights of artists and is the official certification agency for gold, platinum, and multiplatinum sales awards. RIAA publishes the newsletter *Fast Tracks*.

Songwriters Guild of America (SGA)
209 Tenth Ave. South, Ste. 321
Nashville, TN 37203
(615) 742-9945
fax: (615) 742-9948
e-mail: nash@songwritersguild.com
Web site: www.songwritersguild.com

SGA is a songwriters' association that advocates on issues of importance to songwriters and the music industry in general, including home taping, derivative rights, authors' moral rights, and infringement of royalty payment due to digital/Internet piracy. The group works on lobbying, talking with the media, and negotiating and coordinating with other industry groups. SGA publishes the newsletter *Songwriters Guild of America*.

For Further Reading

Books

Bordowitz, Hank. *Dirty Little Secrets of the Record Business: Why So Much Music You Hear Sucks.* Chicago: Chicago Review, 2007.

Kalliongis, Nicky. *MySpace Music Profit Monster! Proven Online Marketing Strategies.* New York: MTV, 2008.

Keith, Michael C. *The Radio Station: Broadcast, Satellite and Internet.* Burlington, MA: Focal, 2006.

Kusek, Dave, and Gerd Leonhard. *The Future of Music: Manifesto for the Digital Music Revolution.* Boston: Berklee, 2005.

Litman, Jessica. *Digital Copyright: Protecting Intellectual Property on the Internet.* Amherst, NY: Prometheus, 2001.

Marmorstein, Gary. *The Label: The Story of Columbia Records.* New York: Da Capo, 2007.

Menn, Joseph. *All the Rave: The Rise and Fall of Shawn Fanning's Napster.* New York: Crown Business, 2003.

Mewton, Conrad. *All You Need to Know About Music and the Internet Revolution.* London: Sanctuary, 2005.

Milano, Brett. *Vinyl Junkies: Adventures in Record Collecting.* New York, St. Martin's Griffin, 2003.

Reid, Antonio "LA," et al. *Inside the Minds: The Music Business—CEOs and Presidents from Island Def Jam, LLC, EMI Music, North Group and More Provide a Behind the Scenes Glimpse into Recording, Promotions and Entertainment.* Boston: Aspatore, 2004.

Shaw, Russell, and Dave Mercer. *Caution! Music and Video Downloading: Your Guide to Legal, Safe and Trouble-Free Downloads.* Hoboken, NJ: Wiley, 2004.

Periodicals

Adams, Steve. "Vinyl Records Gain Popularity Among Audiophiles, iPod Generation," *Lincoln Courier*, April 26, 2008. www.lincolncourier .com/archive/x1611215838.

Aristotle, Rick. "The Day Internet Radio Died," *Motley Fool,* June 26, 2007. www.fool.com/investing/general/2007/06/26/the-day-internet-radio-died.aspx.

Byrne, David. "David Byrne's Survival Strategies for Emerging Artists—and Megastars," *Wired,* December 18, 2007. www.wired.com/entertainment/music/magazine/16-01/ff_byrne.

Dahlen, Chris. "Opinion: Transcendental Air Guitar—Why Games and Music Need Each Other," *Gamasutra,* March 21, 2008. www.gamasutra.com/php-bin/news_index.php?story=17805.

Durcholz, Nick. "Download This: Music Should Be Available for Mass Audiences," *USI Shield,* August 9, 2008. www.usishield.com/2.4776/1.457623.

Feld, Harold. "CD Sales Dead? Not for Indies!" *Public Knowledge,* March 27, 2007. www.publicknowledge.org/node/890.

Fine, Jon. "Leaving Record Labels Behind," *Business Week,* October 29, 2007. www.businessweek.com/magazine/content/07_44/b4056094.htm.

Fisher, Marc. "Download Uproar: Record Industry Goes After Personal Use," *Washington Post,* December 30, 2007. www.washingtonpost.com/wp-dyn/content/article/2007/12/28/AR2007122800693.html.

Hanson, Kurt, and Jay Rosenthal. "Can the Music Industry Suc Its Way to Profit?" *Los Angeles Times,* June 15, 2007. www.latimes.com/news/opinion/la-op-dustup15jun15,0,43795.story.

———. "Web Spinners and Royalty Collectors," *Los Angeles Times,* June 11, 2007. www.latimes.com/news/opinion/la-op-dustup-11jun11,0,6208772.story?coll=la-opinion-center.

McMurty, James. "High-Fidelity Memories on Record Store Day," *NPR Music,* April 19, 2008. www.npr.org/templates/story/story.php?storyId=89774100.

Mother_Road. "Satellite Radio Is My Travel Killer App," Disney Family.com, March 26, 2007. http://family.go.com/blog/mother_road/satellite-radio-is-my-travel-killer-app-226696.

Riemenschneider, Chris. "R.I.P. the CD 1982–2007," *Minneapolis Star-Tribune,* January 25, 2008. www.startribune.com/entertainment/music/14294271.html.

Smith, Ethan. "Sales of Music, Long in Decline, Plunge Sharply," *Wall Street Journal*, March 21, 2007. http://online.wsj.com/article/ SB117444575607043728.html?mod=todays_us_page_one.

Swihart, Jonathan. "Fight the Power: Downloading to Empower Artists," *Campus Press*, March 12, 2007. http://media.www.thecampuspress .com/media/storage/paper1098/news/2007/03/12/Opinion/Fight .The.Power.Downloading.To.Empower.Artists-2772841.shtml.

Index

Picture Credits

Daniel Acker/Bloomberg News/Landov, 32

AP Images, 37, 97, 104

Abby Brack/Getty Images, 60

Autumn Cruz/MCT/Landov, 120

Shaun Curry/AFP/Getty Images, 10

Chip East/Reuters/Landov, 20

Gary Gershoff/WireImage, 46

Pat Greenhouse/Boston Globe/Landov, 44

Rob Kim/Landov, 114

Steve Marcus/Reuters/Landov, 57

Yui Mok/PA Photos/Landov, 80

Newhouse News Service/Landov, 124

© Nordicphotos/Alamy, 25

Andre Padilla, 14, 18, 27, 31, 38, 42, 51, 55, 61, 65, 74, 78, 87, 91, 99, 109, 115, 119, 127

© Photononstop/SuperStock, 85

Claude Prigent/Maxppp/Landov, 92

Jason Reed/Reuters/Landov, 49

© Helene Rogers/Alamy, 13

Shannon Stapleton/Reuters/Landov, 110

© Stocksearch/Alamy, 69, 82

Abel Uribe/MCT/Landov, 73